Make That Grade
Accounting Revision

ormation ..

'ord, Dublin 1

)78513 Fax ...

iibrary@im:

http·''

Make That Grade Accounting Revision

Tommy Robinson

Gill & Macmillan

Gill & Macmillan Ltd
Goldenbridge
Dublin 8
with associated companies throughout the world
© Tommy Robinson 1999

0 7171 2510 6

Print origination by Mathematical Composition Setters Ltd, Salisbury, Wiltshire

Printed by ColourBooks Ltd, Dublin

A catalogue record is available for this book from the British Library.

5 4 3 2 1

Contents

Preface

This book has been designed to provide students with a bank of questions and answers to help them learn accounting and, later, to revise what they have learned before exams. It should be useful to third level students undertaking courses in business or accounting, both as part of a business/accounting degree or as part of a broader degree or other qualification. As much of the Leaving Certificate Accounting syllabus is covered, it should also be of help to students studying that subject.

The book will be especially useful to students preparing for the following professional examinations:

- The Institute of Chartered Accountants in Ireland – Professional One – Introduction to Accounting
- The Institute of Accounting Technicians in Ireland – Foundation Examination Accounts 1
- The Institute of Certified Public Accountants in Ireland – Formation 1 – Accounting
- The Chartered Association of Certified Accountants – Paper 1 – The Accounting Framework.

Past examination questions from all the bodies named, for the above and other papers, are included throughout the book. I thank them and also the Institute of Taxation in Ireland, the Institute of Bankers in Ireland, the Association of Accounting Technicians, the Chartered Institute of Management Accountants and the Institute of Chartered Secretaries and Administrators for granting me permission to reproduce questions from their examination papers. I accept full responsibility for any errors, whether in the suggested solutions to these or other questions.

I thank my friends, colleagues and others, too numerous to mention, for their advice and assistance. I trust that they will not be offended by my inability to list them all here. I thank, also, the many students who, through their insightful questioning, have contributed to the book.

Tommy Robinson
November 1998

Part 1
Questions

Section 1

The Trial Balance, Accounting Concepts, Capital and Revenue Expenditure

Question 1.1

Outline the various types of errors that might remain in a business' nominal ledger even if the Trial Balance is extracted from the ledger balances.

(Suggested Solution on Page 93)

Question 1.2

What are Fundamental Accounting Concepts?

(Suggested Solution on Page 94)

Question 1.3

Explain the meaning of the four fundamental accounting concepts referred to in SSAP 2 and indicate in what order of priority they rank.

(Suggested Solution on Page 94)

Question 1.4

Explain the term 'accounting bases'.

(Suggested Solution on Page 95)

Question 1.5

Explain the term 'accounting policies'.

(Suggested Solution on Page 95)

Question 1.6

Explain why accounting policies should be disclosed.

(Suggested Solution on Page 96)

Question 1.7

Outline the nature of capital expenditure.

(Suggested Solution on Page 96)

Question 1.8

Outline the nature of revenue expenditure.

(Suggested Solution on Page 96)

Question 1.9

Outline the reasons for the distinction between capital expenditure and revenue expenditure.

(Suggested Solution on Page 96)

Section 2

Depreciation

Question 2.1

Explain what is meant by the term 'depreciation'.

(Suggested Solution on Page 97)

Question 2.2

Critically evaluate the statement that the purpose of depreciation is to provide for the replacement of fixed assets.

(Suggested Solution on Page 97)

Question 2.3

Explain why it was considered necessary to introduce an accounting standard concerning depreciation.

(Suggested Solution on Page 98)

Question 2.4

Why should buildings be depreciated even though they may be appreciating (increasing) in value?

(Suggested Solution on Page 98)

Question 2.5

Why should the cost of leasehold land be depreciated but the cost of freehold land not be depreciated?

(Suggested Solution on Page 98)

Question 2.6

Your firm's client, Thompson Ltd., has provided you with the following information in relation to its fixed assets for 1996.

Balances as at 1 January	*Plant*	*Vehicles*
Cost	£194,000	£58,000
Provision for Depreciation	82,000	30,000
Depreciation Rates (Straight Line)	20%	20%
Additions During the Year	£38,000	£20,000
Assets Disposed of During the Year		
Cost	£21,000	£25,000
Proceeds	£8,000	£7,200
Year of Acquisition	1994	1992

A full year's depreciation is provided in the year of purchase and none in the year of sale.

Required

(a) calculate the cost of fixed assets owned at the end of the year;
(b) calculate the provision for depreciation on fixed assets owned at the end of the year; and
(c) calculate the profit earned and/or loss incurred on fixed assets disposed of during the year.

(Suggested Solution on Page 99)

Question 2.7

At the beginning of its financial year, on 1 June 1996, a firm had a balance on its Plant Account of £84,000 and on its Provision for Depreciation of Plant Account a balance of £32,000. The firm provides for depreciation, using the reducing balance method, on fixed assets held at the end of its financial year at the rate of 20% per annum.

On 31 December 1996 the firm sold a machine which, on 1 February 1993, had cost £16,000 and on which installation charges had totalled £1,000. The cost of transporting this machine to the premises had been £3,000. The proceeds of sale were £10,000. In August 1995, substantial repairs to this machine had cost £3,500. In September 1995 an additional part costing £5,000 had been fitted to this machine in order to improve its performance.

On 1 January 1997 the firm bought second-hand plant costing £24,000, installation costs were £4,000 and the cost of repairs to put the machine into working order were £6,000.

Prepare, for the year ended 31 May 1997:

(a) the Plant Account;
(b) the Provision for Depreciation of Plant Account; and
(c) the Profit and Loss on Disposal of Plant Account.

(Suggested Solution on Page 100)

Question 2.8

At the beginning of its financial year, on 1 January 1995, J. Sedgewick & Co. had a balance on its Machinery Account of £150,000 and a balance on its Provision for Depreciation of Machinery Account of £30,000. The firm provides for depreciation at the rate of 10% on fixed assets held at the end of its financial year, using the reducing balance method.

On 31 March 1995 the firm sold a machine which had cost them £24,000 on 30 September, 1991. Installation charges on this machine were £4,000 and the cost of transporting it to the premises was £2,000. In April 1993 substantial repairs to this machine had cost £5,000. In May 1993 an additional part was fitted to the machine in order to improve its performance. This cost £6,000. The sale proceeds were £29,000.

On 30 June 1996 the firm bought a second-hand machine for £10,000. Installation costs were £2,000 and transport costs were £1,000. It was discovered that this machine was unsuitable for its intended purpose and, on 30 September 1996, it was sold for £8,000. The cost of dismantling it and transporting it to the buyer was £2,000.

Required

Prepare for the years ended 31 December 1995 and 1996:

(a) the Machinery Account;
(b) the Provision for Depreciation of Machinery Account; and
(c) the Disposal of Machinery Account.

(Suggested Solution on Page 103)

Question 2.9

Steel Ltd. commenced business on 1 July 1993. On that date it purchased and paid for a rolling machine for £10,000 and a milling machine for £15,000. Each machine had an estimated useful life of 5 years and is not expected to have any scrap value.

On 30 June 1995 Steel Ltd. traded in the milling machine against a new milling machine, the list price of which was £24,000. The company was given a trade-in allowance of £6,000 on its old machine. The new machine had an estimated useful life of 5 years.

On 1 July 1996 the company purchased a new machine which could do the work of its two existing machines. The list price of the new machine was £25,000 and Steel Ltd. was given a trade-in allowance of £15,000 against its old machines. The estimated useful life of the new machine was 5 years.

The financial year of Steel Ltd. ends on 30 June each year. It is the policy of the company to depreciate its fixed assets on a straight line basis.

Required

Show how the above transactions should be recorded in the company's ledger for the period 1 July 1993 to 30 June 1997.

(Suggested Solution on Page 106)

Question 2.10

The following information relates to the fixed assets of Axel Ltd.:

Asset	Date Purchased	Cost
Premises	1 January 1993	£200,000
Plant and Equipment	1 May 1994	80,000
Vehicles	1 June 1995	20,000

Additional Information

1. Premises are depreciated at the rate of 2% per annum on the straight line basis.
2. Plant and equipment is depreciated at the rate of 20% per annum on the reducing balance basis.
3. Vehicles are depreciated at the rate of 20% per annum on the straight line basis.
4. All vehicles were disposed of for £12,000 during 1996.
5. The policy of the company is to provide a full year's depreciation in the year of purchase and none in the year of sale.

Required

Prepare and balance the following accounts for 1996:

(a)   Premises at Cost;
(b)   Plant and Equipment at Cost;
(c)   Vehicles at Cost;
(d)   Provision for Depreciation of Premises;
(e)   Provision for Depreciation of Plant and Equipment;
(f)   Provision for Depreciation of Vehicles; and
(g)   Vehicles Disposal Account.

(Suggested Solution on Page 107)

Question 2.11

What factors should be considered in the assessment of depreciation and its allocation to accounting periods?

(Suggested Solution on Page 109)

Question 2.12

In what circumstances does SSAP 12 'Accounting for Depreciation' permit a change in the method of providing for depreciation?

(Suggested Solution on Page 109)

Question 2.13

In the context of SSAP 12 how should a permanent diminution in the value of a fixed asset be treated?

(Suggested Solution on Page 110)

Question 2.14

How should re-valued fixed assets be depreciated?

(Suggested Solution on Page 110)

Question 2.15

What are the disclosure requirements of SSAP 12?

(Suggested Solution on Page 110)

Section 3

Bad Debts and Provisions for Doubtful Debts

Question 3.1

C. Dickens prepares his accounts up to 31 December each year. The provision for doubtful debts in his accounts at 31 December 1993 was £8,750. Bad Debts written off in 1994 totalled £12,500. Debtors at 31 December 1994 were £135,000. The provision for doubtful debts is to be made equal to 4% of this figure. In addition, a provision for discount on debtors of 2% is to be introduced.

Debtors at 31 December 1995 were £190,000 of which £5,000 is to be written off in respect of debts considered to be bad. A further £3,200 had already been written off during the year. A specific provision of £2,000 is to be made against one customer's account and a general provision for doubtful debts of 4% of remaining debtors is to be carried. The provision for discount on debtors is to remain at 2%.

Debtors at 31 December 1996 were £220,000. Bad Debts written off during the year amounted to £6,500. The account on which the specific provision was previously made is now to be written off as bad to the extent of £1,500. The provisions for doubtful debts and discount on debtors are to be maintained at 4% and 2% respectively.

Required

Show for the years 1994, 1995 and 1996:

(a) the Bad Debts account;
(b) the Provision for Doubtful Debts account;
(c) the Provision for Discount on Debtors account;
(d) relevant extracts from the Profit and Loss Accounts; and
(e) relevant extracts from the Balance Sheets.

(Suggested Solution on Page 111)

Question 3.2

Michael Judge commenced business on 1 April 1994 and prepares his accounts up to 31 March each year.

At 31 March 1995 his Debtors Ledger balances totalled £260,000. He decided to write off £7,500 of this figure for bad debts and to make a provision for doubtful debts of 4% of debtors. He also decided to make a provision for discount on debtors of 2%.

At 31 March 1996 debtors were £264,000, of which £15,000 is to be written-off in respect of debts considered to be bad. A specific provision of £4,000 is to be made against one customer's account and a general provision of 4% of remaining debtors is to be carried. The provision for discount on debtors is to remain at 2%.

At 31 March 1997 debtors were £278,000. The account against which the specific provision was previously made is to be written-off as bad at an amount of £4,000. In addition, a further £9,000 is to be treated as bad. The provisions for doubtful debts and discount on debtors are to be maintained at 4% and 2% respectively.

Required

Show for each of the years ended 31 March 1995, 1996 and 1997:

(a) the Bad Debts Account;
(b) the Provision for Doubtful Debts Account;
(c) the Provision for Discount on Debtors Account;
(d) relevant extracts from the Profit and Loss Accounts; and
(e) relevant extracts from the Balance Sheets.

(Suggested Solution on Page 113)

Question 3.3

John Orange, has been in business for a number of years. The following is an aged analysis of his debtors ledger at 31 December 1996.

	Total	Less Than 1 Month	Over 1 Month	Over 2 Months	Over 3 Months	4 Months and Over
A. Ash	£15,000	£10,000	£5,000	£ —	£ —	£ —
B. Black	14,900	900	4,000	6,000	4,000	—
C. Crimson	13,600	600	6,000	—	—	7,000
D. Dark	18,400	2,400	6,000	6,000	4,000	—
Ebony Ltd.	5,900	—	—	—	—	5,900
	67,800	13,900	21,000	12,000	8,000	12,900

Additional Information in respect of 1996

1. (i)   Provision for bad debts at 1 January   £4,900
    (ii) Bad debts provided for during the year   5,000
    (iii) Bad debts written off during the year   4,500
2. (i)   Ebony Ltd. has gone into liquidation and, as none of this debt is recoverable, it is to be written off in full.
    (ii) The provision for bad debts at 31 December is to be calculated on the following basis:
          Debtors 4 months old and over   30%
          Debtors over 3 months and less than 4 months old   25%
          On all other debtors   5%

Required

(a) You are required, in respect of John Orange, to
    (i)   prepare the provision for bad debts account for 1996;
    (ii) calculate the bad debts profit and loss entries for 1996; and
    (iii) show the entries which will appear in the balance sheet as at 31 December 1996.
(b) Explain briefly what you understand by the prudence concept.

(Suggested Solution on Page 115)

Section 4

Accruals and Prepayments

Question 4.1

Catherine O'Byrne, a grocer, prepares accounts each year to 31 December. Her rent and rates expense is recorded in a single rent and rates account and transferred to the profit and loss account at the year-end as a single figure. Details of quarterly rent payments of £1,200 each and the dates of these payments for 1996 are as follows:

Quarter Ended	Rent Paid
31 December 1995	3 December 1995
31 March 1996	2 January 1996
30 June 1996	29 June 1996
30 September 1996	5 December 1996
31 December 1996	9 January 1997

The payments in respect of rates were as follows:

Half Year Ended	Rates Paid	Amount
31 March 1996	5 January 1996	£720
30 September 1996	3 August 1996	840
31 March 1997	2 December 1996	840

Required

Prepare the combined rent and rates account in the Nominal Ledger of Catherine O'Byrne for 1996.

(Suggested Solution on Page 116)

Question 4.2

Catherine Robinson, whose financial year ends on 30 September, maintains a combined rent and rates account in her nominal ledger. Catherine has leased premises for the past 5 years at an annual rent of £24,000 payable quarterly in arrears on 1 January, 1 April, 1 July and 1 October. On 1 July 1996, the rent was increased from £24,000 per annum to £40,000 per annum. Rates amounted to £15,000 in the year to 31 March 1996, and £18,000 in the year to 31 March 1997.
 Payments made by Catherine were as follows:

Date	Payment Details
27 September 1995	Paid rates for the half year to 31 March 1996.
3 October 1995	Paid rent to 30 September 1995.
5 January 1996	Paid rent.
4 April 1996	Paid rent.
27 May 1996	Paid rates for the half year to 30 September 1996.
10 July 1996	Paid rent.

Required

Write up the rent and rates account as it would appear in Catherine's ledger for the year ended 30 September 1996.

(Suggested Solution on Page 117)

Question 4.3

Jones Ltd. prepares accounts each year to 31 December. The company maintains a combined rent and rates account within its nominal ledger. The company leases its premises on a 35 year lease at an annual rent of £72,000 payable quarterly in advance. The following payments were made by the company during 1996:

Date	Payment Details	Amount
1 February	Paid Rent	£18,000
31 March	Paid Rates for the 6 months to 31 March 1996	12,000
1 May	Paid Rent	18,000
1 August	Paid Rent	21,000
30 September	Paid Rates for the 6 months to 30 September 1996	12,000
1 November	Paid Rent	21,000

Additional Information

1. Rent of £18,000 was paid on 1 November 1995, in respect of the quarter to 31 January 1996.
2. A rent review took place on 31 July 1996, and the annual rent was increased to £84,000 from 1 August 1996.
3. Rates for the year to 30 September 1996 amounted to £24,000, and for the year to 30 September 1997 they will amount to £30,000.

Required

Write up the rent and rates account as it would appear in the Nominal Ledger of Jones Ltd. for 1996.

(Suggested Solution on Page 117)

Question 4.4

Andrew Brown prepares accounts to 31 December each year. He maintains a combined Rent and Rates Account in his ledger. At 1 January 1996, the balances on the Rent and Rates Account were as follows:

Rates Prepaid	(3 months to 31 March 1996)	£2,000
Rent Due	(2 months to 31 December 1995)	4,000

Rent is payable quarterly; rates are payable half yearly. The following payments were made by cheque during 1996.

Date	Payment Details
1 February	Paid rent for the quarter to 31 January 1996
1 May	Paid rates for the half year to 30 September 1996
2 May	Paid rent for the quarter to 30 April 1996
14 August	Paid rent for the quarter to 31 July 1996
12 October	Paid rates for the half year to 31 March 1997
11 November	Paid rent for the quarter to 31 October 1996

Rates were increased by £800 per annum with effect from 1 April 1996. Rent was increased by £2,400 per annum with effect from 1 November 1996.

Required

Draw up the Rent and Rates Account for Andrew Brown for 1996.

(Suggested Solution on Page 118)

Question 4.5

Peter Jones owns a house which is subdivided into three flats. He prepares annual accounts to 31 December. There was no rent owing or prepaid on 1 January 1996. On that date the flats were let at a monthly rent as follows.

Flat 1	*Flat 2*	*Flat 3*
£210 per month	£220 per month	£280 per month

He received the following rental income during the year. All rent is paid directly into Mr. Jones' bank account.

Flat 1	*Flat 2*	*Flat 3*
£3,402	£1,639	£3,640

Flat 1 was occupied for 12 months of the year. Flat 2 was occupied for the first 4 months and the last 6 months of the year. Flat 3 was occupied for the first month and the last 10 months of the year. The rent of the flats increased during the year as follows.

Flat 1	10% from 1 April 1996
Flat 2	15% from 1 July 1996
Flat 3	20% from 1 September 1996

Required

Prepare the rent receivable account of Mr. Jones for 1996.

(Suggested Solution on Page 119)

Question 4.6

International Airlines Ltd. has one large wide-bodied jet aircraft. Transport regulations require that the aircraft be subject to a major overhaul after every 10,000 flying hours. The cost of a major overhaul is estimated at £1,500,000.

It is the company's policy to charge the overhaul expense to accounting periods in proportion to the number of hours flown in each period and, to this end, the company maintains a provision for major overhauls account.

The number of hours flown and the actual overhaul costs paid in each of the years 1993 through 1996 were as follows:

	1993	*1994*	*1995*	*1996*
Hours Flown	5,600	6,200	5,800	6,400
Overhaul Cost Paid	—	£1.5m	—	£1.5m

Required

(a) write up the provision for major overhauls account for each of the years ended 31 December 1993, 1994, 1995 and 1996; and

(b) indicate how any balance on the account would be included in the balance sheet.

(Suggested Solution on Page 120)

Section 5

The Valuation of Stock

Question 5.1

Explain the First In, First Out (FIFO) method of approximating the cost of stock.

(Suggested Solution on Page 121)

Question 5.2

Explain the Last In, First Out (LIFO) method of approximating the cost of stock.

(Suggested Solution on Page 121)

Question 5.3

Explain the Average Cost method of approximating the cost of stock.

(Suggested Solution on Page 121)

Question 5.4

Explain the meaning of 'lower of cost and net realisable value'.

(Suggested Solution on Page 122)

Question 5.5

Explain how stocks of raw materials should be valued, and why.

(Suggested Solution on Page 122)

Question 5.6

Explain how stocks of finished goods should be valued, and why.

(Suggested Solution on Page 122)

Question 5.7

The following stock-related transactions occurred during the period 1 July to 31 December.

Date	Transaction
25 July	Purchased 150 units of stock @ £20 each
28 August	Purchased 225 units of stock @ £30 each
15 September	Sold 305 units of stock @ £45 each
4 October	Sold 50 units of stock @ £45 each
10 November	Purchased 410 units of stock @ £40 each
23 December	Sold 100 units of stock @ £75 each

Additional Information

1. The Balance Sheet as at 1 July was as follows:

Bank	£10,000
Capital Account	£10,000

2. Two months' credit is received from suppliers.
3. One month's credit is allowed to customers.
4. Expenses of £1,400 are paid by cheque each month as incurred.
5. The purchase and sale prices referred to above are exclusive of VAT. Purchases are liable to VAT at the rate of 10% and sales are liable to VAT at the rate of 20%.

Required

(a) calculate the value of stock on hand at the end of each month during the period 1 July to 31 December, using the First In, First Out method (FIFO); and
(b) prepare a Trading and Profit and Loss Account and Balance Sheet for the period 1 July to 31 December.

(Suggested Solution on Page 123)

Section 6

Bank Reconciliation Statements

Question 6.1

The following information relating to the bank account of Joseph Brown has been presented to you:

1 June   Bank balance per nominal ledger (Debit)   £891

Lodgements			Cheque Payments		
Date	*Amount*		*Date*	*Cheque No.*	*Amount*
2 June	£24,819		3 June	500 060	£3,351
5 June	5,769		5 June	500 061	1,314
16 June	7,485		11 June	500 062	26,334
16 June	9,126		15 June	500 063	9,000
21 June	5,784		19 June	500 064	1,770
22 June	1,386		21 June	500 065	2,133
30 June	144		30 June	500 066	1,566

Joseph received the following bank statement for the month of June:

Date	Particulars	£ Debit	£ Credit	£ Balance
June 1	Balance			3,600 Cr.
2	Lodgement		900	
2	Lodgement		24,819	29,319 Cr.
4	Cheque No. 500 059	1,233		28,086 Cr.
5	Cheque No. 500 058	2,376		
5	Cheque No. 500 060	3,351		
5	Lodgement		5,769	28,128 Cr.
16	Lodgement		16,611	44,739 Cr.
21	Cheque No. 500 061	1,314		
21	Cheque No. 500 064	1,770		
21	Lodgement		5,844	47,499 Cr.
22	Cheque No. 500 065	2,133		
22	Lodgement		1,386	46,752 Cr.
25	Standing Order	825		45,927 Cr.
30	Bank Giro Credit Transfer		576	46,503 Cr.

You are informed by the bank that all entries on their statement are correct.

Required

Prepare a statement showing your reconciliation of the closing balance on the bank statement, with the corrected nominal ledger balance at 30 June.

(Suggested Solution on Page 126)

Question 6.2

A client of your firm, Mr. Gerard Knight, has provided you with his Bank Statement showing the following details for the month of December:

Date	Details	Debit	Credit	Balance
		£	£	£
December 1	Balance forward			1,500 Dr.
2	Life Assurance DD	45		
	Cheque 508204	125		
	Cheque 508206	138		
	Lodgement		900	908 Dr.
5	Motor Lease DD	287		
	Cheque 508205	185		
	Cheque 508209	142		
	Lodgement		1,500	22 Dr.
9	Cheque 508207	200		222 Dr.
12	Unpaid Cheque	450		672 Dr.
16	Interest	315		
	Bank Charges	204		1,191 Dr.
19	Lodgement		2,000	809 Cr.
	Cheque 508214	309		500 Cr.
31	Cheque 508213	140		
	Cheque 508215	212		
	Bank Charges	3		145 Cr.

Mr. Knight has also provided you with the bank account in his own records for the month of December, which shows the following:

Dec 2	Lodgement	£900	Dec 1	Balance b/d	£1,810
Dec 9	Lodgement	1,500	Dec 2	Cheque 508206	138
Dec 18	Lodgement	1,890	Dec 4	Cheque 508207	200
			Dec 5	Cheque 508208	350
			Dec 5	Cheque 508209	140
			Dec 6	Cheque 508210	285
			Dec 6	Cheque 508211	487
			Dec 7	Cheque 508212	384
			Dec 16	Cheque 508213	140
			Dec 16	Cheque 508214	390
			Dec 20	Cheque 508215	221
Dec 31	Balance c/d	288	Dec 21	Cheque 508216	33
		4,578			4,578

You are advised that the entries on the Bank Statement are correct.

Required

(a) write up the adjustments in the bank account in Mr. Knight's records; and
(b) prepare the Bank Reconciliation Statement as at 31 December.

(Suggested Solution on Page 127)

Section 7

Control Accounts

Question 7.1

Explain briefly the advantages of preparing control accounts.

(Suggested Solution on Page 128)

Question 7.2

The following information relates to the purchases and sales of Ted Sweeney, a sole trader, for 1996.

Debtors at 1 January 1996	£170,000
Creditors at 1 January 1996	130,000
Sales on Credit	450,000
Purchases on Credit	320,000
Sales Returns	18,000
Purchases Returns	22,000
Receipts from Debtors	410,000
Payments to Creditors	290,000
Discount Allowed to Debtors	16,000
Discount Received from Creditors	25,000
Bad Debts Written Off	14,000

Additional Information

1. The total of the credit balances in the Debtors Ledger at 31 December 1996, was £7,000.
    The total of the debit balances in the Creditors Ledger at 31 December 1996, was £11,000.
2. Sam Smith is both a debtor and creditor of Ted Sweeney and £2,500 due from him, is to be offset against the balance due to him, in the Creditors' Ledger.

Required

Prepare the Debtors and Creditors Control Accounts for Ted Sweeney for 1996.

(Suggested Solution on Page 128)

Question 7.3

The following information relates to the debtors and creditors of Beta Ltd. for 1996:

1. *Balances as at 1 January 1996:*

Debtors' Ledger Debit Balances	£20,000 Dr.
Debtors' Ledger Credit Balances....................................	2,000 Cr.
Creditors' Ledger Credit Balances.................................	18,000 Cr.
Creditors' Ledger Debit Balances.................................	8,000 Dr.

2. *Transactions for 1996:*

Sales on Credit...	£140,000
Sales Returns	8,000
Purchases on Credit...	90,000
Purchases Returns	4,000
Receipts from Debtors...	120,000
Discount Allowed to Debtors......................................	2,000
Bad Debts Written Off	6,000
Payments to Creditors	75,000
Discount Allowed by Creditors....................................	3,000

3. At 31 December 1996 the total of the credit balances in the debtors' ledger was £3,000 and the total of the debit balances in the creditors' ledger was £1,200

Required

Prepare the Debtors' and Creditors' Control Accounts for Beta Ltd. for 1996.

(Suggested Solution on Page 129)

Question 7.4

The Debtors Control Account of M. Twain as at 31 March 1997 showed a balance of £257,200 while the Creditors Control Account showed £191,400. Neither of these balances agreed with the relevant List of Balances. The following errors were discovered, and, when these had been corrected, the ledger and lists agreed.

(a) The Purchases Book had been overcast by £10,000.
(b) Goods worth £750 returned to a supplier had not been entered anywhere in the accounting records.
(c) A credit balance of £250 on the debtors list had been shown as a debit balance.
(d) A bad debt of £800 had been written off in the debtors ledger but no entry had been made in the Control Account.
(e) It had been agreed with J. Kelly to set the balance on his account in the Creditors Ledger of £1,500 against his account in the Debtors Ledger. This had been entered in the Debtors Ledger and in both Control Accounts but was not shown in the Creditors Ledger.
(f) A balance of £1,300 had been omitted from the list of debtors balances.
(g) A purchase of goods from C. Temple of £3,500 had been posted to the wrong side of his ledger account.
(h) A refund of £500 to a customer, A. Smith, had been posted to the credit side of B. Smith's account in the Creditors Ledger.
(i) Discount received of £320 had been entered in the Control Account but not in the Creditors Ledger Account.
(j) The Sales Returns Book had been overcast by £1,000.

Required

1. Calculate the correct balances on the Debtors and Creditors Control Accounts as at 31 March 1997; and
2. Prepare a statement reconciling the original total balances extracted from the ledger with the corrected balance for each ledger

(Suggested Solution on Page 129)

Question 7.5

The Debtors Control Account of D. Swift as at 31 December 1996 showed a balance of £78,214, while the Creditors Control Account showed a balance of £56,191. Neither of these balances agreed with the respective lists of balances. Following investigation the following errors were found:

1. Goods sold on credit to T. Evans for £2,300 had been posted to the wrong side of his ledger account.

2. A bad debt of £600 had been written off in the debtors' ledger account but no entry had been made in the relevant Control Account.
3. £670 owed to a creditor had been omitted from the list of creditors balances.
4. Goods worth £635, returned by a customer, had not been entered anywhere in the accounting records.
5. A refund of £1,200 to a customer, P. Moran, had been posted only to the credit side of P. Moran's account in the creditors ledger.
6. A £90 debit balance on the creditors list had been shown as a credit balance.
7. Discount received of £215 had not been entered anywhere in the accounting records.
8. The Sales Book had been undercast by £1,000.
9. It had been agreed with C. Smith to set the balance on his account in the debtors' ledger of £1,260 against his account in the creditors' ledger. This had been entered in the creditors' ledger and in both control accounts, but was not shown in the debtors' ledger.
10. The Purchases Book had been undercast by £900.

You are required to prepare:

(a) your computation of the corrected balances at 31 December 1996 of the Debtors Control Account and Creditors Control Account; and
(b) a statement reconciling the original total balances extracted from the ledger, with the corrected balance for each ledger.

(Suggested Solution on Page 130)

Question 7.6

The balance on the Debtors Control Account of Trimleaf Ltd. at 31 March 1997, was £17,370, while the total of the list of the balances in the Debtors Ledger was £16,580.
On investigation of the difference, the following items were discovered:

1. A credit balance of £250 on Black's account had been listed as a debit balance.
2. No entry had been made in respect of a contra of £200 (which had been agreed) between Blue's accounts in the Debtors and Creditors ledgers.
3. In June 1996, sales returns of £350 were posted to the Control Account as £530.
4. In August 1996, £11,480 received from debtors was posted to the debit side of the Creditors Control Account, while cheques issued to creditors of £10,170 were posted to the credit side of the Debtors Control Account.
5. A balance of £300 due from White was omitted from the List of Balances.
6. A balance of £470 due from Yellow Ltd. was listed as £740.

7. In January 1997, the debtors column of the Cash Book was wrongly totted as £11,780 and posted to the Control Account. The correct amount should have been £12,460.
8. In February 1997, a debt of £450 was written off as bad. The only entry made to record this was to credit the Debtors Control Account and debit the Bad Debts Account.
9. In March 1997, £100 was received in respect of a debt previously written off as bad. The only entry made to record this was to debit the Bank Account and credit the Debtors Control Account.

Required

Prepare a reconciliation of the balance on the Debtors Control Account with the total of the List of Balances in the Debtors Ledger.

(Suggested Solution on Page 132)

Section 8

Correction of Errors and Suspense Accounts

Question 8.1

In preparing the final accounts of Knight Ltd. for 1996, you have discovered the following items for which adjustments are required:

1. £1,700 received for the sale of fixtures and fittings, which had originally cost £3,400, was debited to the bank account and credited to the sales account. No entries were made in the ledger for the disposal of these fixtures and fittings. The provision for depreciation on the items disposed of amounted to £1,530.
2. £2,800 of direct debits in respect of advertising, which had been included in the bank statement, were excluded from expenses and from the company's bank account.
3. £4,800 received from a debtor of the company was treated incorrectly as a cash sale.

4. Goods purchased for £3,800 had been returned to suppliers in December 1996. No entries were made in the company's ledger to reflect this transaction.

Required

(a) draft the journal entries to post the above adjustments; and
(b) assuming that a net profit of £7,800 had been calculated before the discovery of the above adjustments, calculate the revised profit figure.

(Suggested Solution on Page 133)

Question 8.2

The draft Financial Statements of Thomas Keynes for the year ended 31 January 1997 showed a net loss of £2,800. During the audit of these accounts the following errors were discovered. A Suspense Account had been opened to record the net difference in the Trial Balance.

1. A fixed asset which had cost £2,500 was posted to Repairs. Depreciation was charged on this asset at the rate of 10% of cost.
2. An accrual for Bank Interest and Charges of £1,400, and a prepayment for Insurance of £600 at 31 January 1996, had not been brought down as opening balances.
3. A Value Added Tax credit of £500 on Motor Expenses had been incorrectly claimed and must be repaid to the Revenue Commissioners.
4. Mr. Keynes took stock costing £1,200 for his personal use. No entry had been made in the accounts for this.
5. Capital introduced by Mr. Keynes of £5,000 had been entered correctly in the Cash Book but was debited to Sales.
6. A prepayment on Rent Payable of £850 at 31 January 1997 had been omitted from the accounts.
7. A contra entry between the Sales Ledger and the Purchases Ledger of £2,500 had been correctly entered in the Purchases Ledger but was omitted from the Sales Ledger.
8. Trade debtors were shown as £57,800. However,
   (a) Bad Debts of £3,800 had not been written off;
   (b) the existing provision for doubtful debts of £3,400 should have been shown as 5% of debtors; and
   (c) a provision for discount on debtors of 2% should have been raised.

Required

(a) prepare a statement correcting the net loss; and
(b) complete the Suspense Account.

(Suggested Solution on Page 134)

Question 8.3

The draft Financial Statements of Paul Benton, for the year ended 31 March 1997, showed a net profit of £13,360. During the audit of these accounts the following errors were discovered. A Suspense Account had been opened to record the net difference in the draft accounts.

(a) Capital introduced by Mr. Benton of £12,000 had been entered correctly in the Cash Book but had been debited to drawings.

(b) A fixed asset which had cost £7,500 was posted to the Purchases account. Depreciation is calculated at the rate of 10% of cost.

(c) An insurance prepayment of £1,500 at 31 March 1996 had not been brought down as an opening balance.

(d) No adjustment had been made to either the Creditors' Ledger or the relevant discount account for discount of £650 which had been granted.

(e) Trade Debtors were shown as £36,600. However,
  (i)   Bad Debts of £2,600 had not been written off.
  (ii) The existing provision for doubtful debts of £2,000 should have been adjusted to 5% of debtors.
  (iii) A provision of 2% for discount on debtors should have been raised.

(f) A contra entry between the Sales Ledger and the Purchases Ledger of £1,000 had been correctly entered in the Sales Ledger but was omitted from the Purchases Ledger.

(g) Credit Sales of £2,500 had been correctly credited to the Sales Account but had been debited to the customer's account as £250.

(h) On 31 March 1997 both an accrual of £1,300 for bank interest, and a rent prepayment of £800, had been omitted from the accounts.

Required

1. Prepare a statement correcting the net profit; and
2. Complete the Suspense Account.

(Suggested Solution on Page 136)

Section 9

Final Accounts of Sole Traders

Question 9.1

The Trial Balance of J. Charleton as at 31 March 1997 was as follows:

	£ Debit	£ Credit
Premises	220,000	
Vehicles at cost	56,000	
Provision for depreciation on vehicles		11,200
Equipment at cost	24,000	
Provision for depreciation on equipment		7,200
Stock on hand as at 1 April 1996	74,000	
Debtors	85,000	
Bank		16,250
Creditors		43,500
Sales		750,000
Purchases	465,000	
Wages and Salaries	87,000	
Motor Expenses	26,500	
Telephone and Postage	8,600	
Light and Heat	17,410	
Rates	6,900	
Insurance	13,400	
Bank Interest and Charges	18,950	
Legal Fees	15,000	
Accountancy Charges	3,200	
Rent		12,000
Value Added Tax	2,200	
Miscellaneous Expenses	8,470	
Drawings	20,600	
Capital		162,080
Bank Loan (Long-term)		150,000
	1,152,230	1,152,230

Notes

1. Depreciation is to be charged on the cost of fixed assets at the following annual rates:
   Vehicles   20%
   Equipment   10%
2. Stock on hand at 31 March 1997 was valued at £68,000.
3. 'Value Added Tax' represents a refund due from the Revenue Commissioners at 31 March 1997.
4. 'Legal Fees' includes £12,500 which relates to the purchase of the premises. A further £5,000 is due in relation to this transaction.
5. Part of the premises was let on 1 January 1997 at a rent of £12,000 per annum, payable in advance.
6. Insurance prepaid as at 31 March 1997 amounted to £2,200.
7. Amounts due but unpaid as at 31 March 1997 were:
   Bank Interest   £5,600
   Miscellaneous Expenses   £4,200
8. Bad debts of £5,500 are to be written off. A provision of 2% of remaining debtors is to be made.

You are required to prepare:

(a) a Trading and Profit and Loss Account for the year ended 31 March 1997; and
(b) a Balance Sheet as at 31 March 1997.

(Suggested Solution on Page 138)

Question 9.2

Pat O'Neill is a sole trader. The following trial balance was extracted from his ledger at 31 December 1996:

	£ Debit	£ Credit
Sales		550,000
Purchases	300,000	
Wages	80,000	
Rent and rates	5,000	
Insurance...	8,000	
Motor travel..	12,000	
Repairs and renewals...	11,000	
Bank interest and charges	3,000	
Bad debts	9,000	
Plant and equipment at cost....................................	75,000	
Provision for depreciation on plant and equipment.....		27,000
Debtors...	90,000	
Bank..	75,000	
Stock on hand at 1 January 1996 (at cost)	50,000	
Creditors...		40,000
Capital..		116,000
Drawings...	15,000	
	733,000	733,000

Additional Information

1. Stock on hand at 31 December 1996 was valued at £65,000.
2. Depreciation is to be provided on plant and equipment at the rate of 20% per annum using the reducing balance method.
3. A provision for bad debts equal to 15% of debtors is to be created.
4. Provision has not been made for bank interest and charges amounting to £800, due to the bank at 31 December 1996.

Required

(a) prepare the Trading and Profit and Loss Account of Pat O'Neill for 1996; and
(b) prepare the Balance Sheet as at 31 December 1996.

(Suggested Solution on Page 140)

Question 9.3

The Trial Balance of B. Harton as at 31 December 1996 was as follows:

	£ Debit	£ Credit
Capital		165,000
Bank Loan (Long-term)		100,000
Plant and equipment at cost	40,000	
Provision for depreciation on plant and equipment		4,000
Vehicles at cost	60,000	
Provision for depreciation on vehicles		12,000
Office Equipment at cost	8,000	
Provision for depreciation on office equipment		800
Stock on hand on 1 January 1996	180,000	
Debtors	114,000	
Provision for Doubtful Debts		1,500
Creditors		76,000
Bank		34,500
Sales		746,000
Rental income		7,400
Purchases	556,000	
Wages	68,000	
Rent and Rates	24,000	
Motor Expenses	16,000	
Insurance	7,600	
Telephone and Postage	8,400	
Light and Heat	6,200	
Bank Interest and Charges	12,800	
Accountancy Charges	3,500	
Income Tax Paid	10,000	
Miscellaneous Expenses	12,400	
Value Added Tax	4,800	
PAYE/PRSI		6,300
Drawings	21,800	
	1,153,500	1,153,500

Notes

1. Depreciation is to be charged on the cost of fixed assets at the following annual rates:
   Plant and Equipment, and Office Equipment   10%
   Vehicles   20%
2. Stock on hand at 31 December 1996 was valued at £160,000.

3. Amounts due but unpaid at 31 December 1996 were:
   Accountancy Charges   £1,500
   Miscellaneous Expenses   £2,300
4. Amounts prepaid at 31 December 1996 were:
   Rent expense   £6,000
   Rental income   £1,200
5. Amounts shown for PAYE/PRSI and Value Added Tax represent balances due to, or from, the Revenue Commissioners.
6. Bad debts of £6,000 are to be written off. A provision for doubtful debts of 2.5% is to be carried.

You are required to prepare:

(a) a Trading and Profit and Loss Account for 1996; and
(b) a Balance Sheet as at 31 December 1996.

(Suggested Solution on Page 142)

Question 9.4

The following Trial Balance was extracted from the ledger of T. Hardy on 31 December 1996.

	£ Debit	£ Credit
Sales		610,000
Purchases	385,000	
Wages and Salaries	48,000	
Telephone and Postage	10,700	
Motor Expenses	18,400	
Rent and Rates	13,240	
Light and Heat	11,470	
Insurance	14,150	
Bank Interest and Charges	9,100	
Accountancy Fees	2,460	
General Expenses	8,190	
Value Added Tax	3,240	
PAYE/PRSI	34,700	
Stock on hand on 1 January 1996	37,200	
Debtors	27,400	
Creditors		49,280
Bank		13,740
Vehicles at cost	48,000	
Provision for depreciation of vehicles		9,600
Equipment at cost	16,000	
Provision for depreciation of equipment		4,800
Drawings	18,750	
Capital		18,580
	706,000	706,000

Notes

1. Depreciation is to be charged on the cost of fixed assets at the following annual rates:
   Vehicles   20%
   Equipment   10%
2. Stock on hand on 31 December 1996 was valued at £28,500.
3. Amounts due but unpaid at 31 December 1996 were:
   Telephone and Postage   £1,500
   Bank Interest and Charges   £800
4. Rent Prepaid as at 31 December 1996 was £2,400
5. £2,400 is to be written off debtors in respect of bad debts. In addition, a provision for doubtful debts of 5% of debtors is to be made.

6. In relation to PAYE/PRSI:
   (a) The figure shown represents payments to the Revenue Commissioners and includes Mr. Hardy's personal income tax liability of £8,000.
   (b) £2,500 remains due and unpaid at 31 December 1996.
   (c) The Profit and Loss charge is to be included in 'Wages and Salaries' which have been shown net in the Trial Balance.
7. 'Value Added Tax' represents a refund due from the Revenue Commissioners at 31 December 1996. Subsequent to the balancing date the Revenue Commissioners correctly disallowed £1,200 of this figure as relating to non-allowable motor expenses.

You are required to prepare:

(a) a Trading and Profit and Loss Account for 1996; and
(b) a Balance Sheet as at 31 December 1996.

(Suggested Solution on Page 144)

Question 9.5

The following Trial Balance was extracted from the ledger of Tony Coakley on 31 March 1997:

	£ Debit	£ Credit
Capital		43,450
Vehicles at cost	66,000	
Provision for depreciation of vehicles		13,200
Fixtures and fittings at cost	15,600	
Provision for depreciation of fixtures and fittings		1,560
Office equipment at cost	6,700	
Provision for depreciation of office equipment		670
Sales		510,000
Purchases	310,800	
Stock on hand on 1 April 1996	27,200	
Wages and Salaries	37,470	
Motor Expenses	15,470	
Rent and Rates	5,950	
Telephone and Postage	2,190	
Light and Heat	4,010	
Repairs and Renewals	1,750	
Insurance	2,460	
Bank Interest and Charges	2,140	
Stationery and Advertising	3,430	
Accountancy Charges	1,570	
Drawings	18,400	
Taxation	48,950	
Trade Debtors	51,400	
Trade Creditors		43,200
Bank		9,410
	621,490	621,490

Additional Information

1. Depreciation is to be charged on the cost of fixed assets at the following annual rates:
   Vehicles   20%
   Fixtures and Fittings   10%
   Office Equipment   10%
2. Stock on hand on 31 March 1997 was valued at £29,500.
3. Insurance prepaid at 31 March 1997 was £660.

4. 'Taxation' comprises the following:

Mr. Coakley's Personal Income Tax Paid	£9,600
Value Added Tax Paid	22,650
PAYE/PRSI Paid	16,700
	48,950

5. The amount shown above for Value Added Tax paid is made up as follows:

VAT on Sales		£76,300
Less		
VAT on Purchases	£53,200	
VAT on Stationary and Advertising	450	53,650
		22,650

6. PAYE/PRSI is to be included in the figure for wages and salaries. £1,500 is due and unpaid at 31 March 1997.
7. Expenses due but unpaid at 31 March 1997 were:

Bank Interest and Charges	£660
Accountancy Charges	£550

8. Bad Debts totalling £4,400 are to be written off and a provision of 2.5% of debtors is to be made in respect of doubtful debts.

You are required to prepare:

(a) a Trading and Profit and Loss Account for the year ended 31 March 1997; and
(b) a Balance Sheet as at 31 March 1997.

(Suggested Solution on Page 146)

Section 10

Final Accounts of Companies

Question 10.1

The following trial balance was extracted from the ledger of Keogh Ltd. at 31 December 1996:

	£ Debit	£ Credit
Ordinary share capital (150,000 shares of 50p each fully paid)..		75,000
12% Preference share capital (80,000 shares of 25p each fully paid)...		20,000
Profit and loss account at 1 January 1996.................		105,000
Premises at cost...	220,000	
Provision for depreciation on premises at 1 January 1996		44,000
Debtors and prepayments	80,000	
Bank current account	25,000	
Stock on hand on 1 January 1996.............................	60,000	
Creditors and accruals		95,000
Sales..		286,000
Purchases..	160,000	
Wages	30,000	
Rent and rates	5,000	
Administration expenses...	15,000	
Selling and distribution expenses..............................	18,000	
Bank interest and charges	4,000	
Bad debts	8,000	
	625,000	625,000

Additional Information

1. Stock on hand on 31 December 1996 was valued at £85,000.
2. Rates of £6,000 in respect of 1996 were due at 31 December 1996, and were not provided for.
3. Depreciation is to be provided on premises at the rate of 2% on cost.
4. A dividend of 10p per ordinary share is to be provided for.
5. The preference share dividend due for the year is to be provided for.

You are required to prepare:

(a) the Trading and Profit and Loss Account of Keogh Ltd. for 1996;
(b) the Profit and Loss Appropriation Account for 1996; and
(c) the Balance Sheet as at 31 December 1996.

(Suggested Solution on Page 148)

Question 10.2

The following Trial Balance was extracted from the ledger of Robin Ltd., after a draft Profit and Loss Account for 1996 had been prepared.

	£ Debit	£ Credit
Premises at cost	200,000	
Provision for depreciation on premises		40,000
Vehicles at cost	35,000	
Provision for depreciation on vehicles		7,000
Debtors and prepayments	130,000	
Stock on hand on 31 December 1996	90,000	
Bank		33,000
Creditors and accruals		80,000
20% Debentures 2001		30,000
Ordinary share capital (62,500 issued shares of 40p each)		25,000
Preference share capital (100,000 issued shares of 50p each)		50,000
General reserve		24,000
Net profit for 1996, before adjustments		79,000
Profit and loss account at 1 January 1996		87,000
	455,000	455,000

Additional Information

1. The following items, which require adjustments to the net profit, have been discovered in a review of the Trial Balance.
    (i)   Stock which cost £25,000 has been found to have a net realisable value of £18,000.
    (ii) A vehicle costing £5,000 has been incorrectly charged to repairs and renewals. This vehicle is to be depreciated at the rate of 20% per annum using the straight line method.
    (iii) An additional PAYE provision of £6,000 is required for salaries paid to directors.
2. Debenture interest is to be provided for.

3. The following dividends have been proposed.
   Ordinary shares   5p per share
   Preference shares   10%
4. £15,000 is to be transferred to the general reserve.

You are required to prepare for Robin Ltd.:

(a) a statement showing the revised net profit for 1996;
(b) the Profit and Loss Appropriation Account for 1996; and
(c) the Balance Sheet as at 31 December 1996.

(Suggested Solution on Page 150)

Question 10.3

The following trial balance was extracted from the ledger of Timber Ltd., as at 31 March 1997:

	Debit £'000	Credit £'000
Ordinary share capital (£1 shares)		1,500
Profit and loss account as at 1 April 1996		870
Buildings at cost	1,800	
Provision for depreciation of buildings		450
Plant and machinery at cost	1,500	
Provision for depreciation of plant and machinery		720
Vehicles at cost	900	
Provision for depreciation of vehicles		540
Stock on hand on 31 March 1997	780	
Debtors	750	
Creditors		630
Bank		90
Sales		5,120
Cost of sales	2,880	
Wages and salaries	450	
Distribution costs	120	
Administration expenses	180	
Rent and rates	180	
Heat and light		
Insurance	240	
Advertising	50	
Provision for bad debts at 1 April 1996		30
Interim dividend paid	90	
	9,950	9,950

Additional Information

1. Due to an error on the stock sheets, the value of the stock on hand on 31 March 1997 has been understated by £80,000.
2. No record was made of goods purchased on credit for £120,000 on 30 March 1997, as the goods were not delivered until 2 April 1997.
3. Bad debts of £30,000 are to be written off and the provision for bad debts is to be adjusted to 5% of debtors.
4. The rent on the company's showrooms has been paid up to 31 January 1997. The cost of renting the showrooms is £18,000 per annum.
5. In March 1997, the company paid rates of £25,000 for the half year to 30 September 1997.
6. In April 1996, the company sold an old vehicle for £20,000. This vehicle had originally cost £30,000 and it had a book value at the date of sale of £15,000. The only entry made in the ledger in respect of this transaction was to debit the bank account, and credit the sales account, with the £20,000 received.
7. Depreciation is to be provided on the cost of fixed assets on hand at 31 March 1997, at the following annual rates:
   Buildings   2%
   Plant and machinery   10%
   Vehicles   20%
8. Provision is to be made for a final dividend of 10%.

Required

(a) prepare the Trading and Profit and Loss Account and the Profit and Loss Appropriation Account for Timber Ltd. for the year ended 31 March 1997; and
(b) prepare the Balance Sheet as at that date.

(Suggested Solution on Page 152)

Question 10.4

The following trial balance was extracted from the ledger of Caruth Ltd. at 31 December 1996:

	£ Debit	£ Credit
Land	200,000	
Buildings at cost...	200,000	
Provision for depreciation of buildings..................		20,000
Plant and machinery at cost		120,000
Provision for depreciation of plant and machinery .		25,000
Vehicles at cost		80,000
Provision for depreciation of vehicles....................		15,000
Stock on hand on 1 January 1996.........................	60,000	
Trade debtors and creditors	120,000	135,000
Bank	15,000	
Ordinary share capital (£1 shares fully paid)..........		200,000
10% preference share capital (£1 shares)		100,000
10% debentures 2001...		60,000
Profit and loss account at 1 January 1996		178,000
Sales..		890,000
Purchases...	620,000	
Wages and salaries	95,000	
Rent...	12,000	
Advertising	40,000	
Printing and stationery	14,000	
Professional fees...	28,000	
Telephone and fax...	22,000	
Provision for bad debts..		8,000
Preference dividend paid	5,000	
	1,631,000	1,631,000

Additional Information

1. Stock on hand on 31 December 1996 was valued at £80,000.
2. During the year a van was bought for £20,000; this amount was posted to the purchases account. Also included in purchases was £1,500 which related to alterations to provide more space for storage in the interior of the van.
3. Depreciation is to be provided on fixed assets on hand at 31 December 1996, as follows:
   Buildings   2% on cost
   Plant and machinery 10% on written down value
   Vehicles   20% on written down value

It is the company's policy to charge a full year's depreciation on assets in the year of purchase, regardless of the date of purchase, and none in the year of sale.

4. During 1995 a debt of £4,000 owing by Dawson Ltd. was written off. On 30 December 1996, Dawson Ltd. indicated that, following an upturn in the company's fortunes, it would be in a position to repay the full amount of the debt on 2 January 1997. The recovery of this bad debt has not been reflected in the trial balance.
5. No debenture interest was paid during the year.
6. Provision is to be made for the final dividend on preference shares and an ordinary dividend of 5p per share.
7. Directors' fees of £30,000 have not yet been provided for.
8. Annual rent amounts to £8,000. Rent has been paid up to 30 June 1997.

Required

(a) prepare the Trading and Profit and Loss Account and the Profit and Loss Appropriation Account for Caruth Ltd. for 1996; and
(b) prepare the Balance Sheet as at 31 December 1996.

(Suggested Solution on Page 154)

Question 10.5

The trial balance of Hall Ltd. on 31 May 1997 was presented as follows:

	£ Debit	£ Credit
Sales		610,000
Cost of sales	420,000	
Stock on hand on 31 May 1997	220,000	
Wages and salaries	84,000	
Rent, rates and insurance	1,200	
Directors' remuneration	4,000	
Administration expenses	7,100	
Debenture interest	1,600	
Light and heat	2,400	
Audit fees	1,500	
Preference dividend	1,000	
Interim ordinary dividend	2,000	
Ordinary share capital		200,000
10% preference share capital		20,000
Profit and loss account as at 1 June 1996		9,400
Bank		6,400
10% debentures 2002		50,000
Machinery at cost	200,000	
Provision for depreciation of machinery		73,000
Vehicles at cost	25,000	
Provision for depreciation of vehicles		10,000
Debtors and creditors	53,000	42,000
Provision for bad debts		2,000
	1,022,800	1,022,800

Additional Information

1. Audit fees of £2,000 in respect of the audit for the year ended 31 May 1997 have not been paid at the end of the year.
2. During the year rates of £600 for the year ended 30 November 1997 were paid.
3. Machinery costing £4,000 with a book-value of £1,700 was sold during the year for £2,800. This amount has not yet been received and no record has been made of this transaction.

4. Depreciation is to be provided on fixed assets at the following annual rates, with a full year's depreciation being provided in the year of acquisition and none in the year of sale.
   Machinery   20% on cost
   Vehicles   20% on book-value
5. Provision is to be made for the preference dividend due and a dividend of 3p per share on the ordinary shares.
6. Bad debts of £1,800 are to be written off and the provision for bad debts is to be maintained at 5% of net trade debtors.
7. Administration expenses include £1,000 paid to a director by way of an interest-free short-term loan.
8. The authorised share capital consists of £600,000 divided into 800,000 ordinary shares of 50p each and 200,000 10% cumulative preference shares of £1 each.

You are required to prepare:

(a) the Trading and Profit and Loss Account and Profit and Loss Appropriation Account for the year ended 31 May 1997; and
(b) a Balance Sheet as at that date.

(Suggested Solution on Page 156)

Question 10.6

The following trial balance was extracted from the ledger of Candles Ltd. as at 31 May 1997.

	Debit £'000	Credit £'000
Ordinary share capital (£1 shares)		500
Profit and loss account as at 1 June 1996		290
Land and buildings at cost	600	
Provision for depreciation of land and buildings		150
Plant and machinery at cost	500	
Provision for depreciation of plant and machinery		240
Vehicles at cost	299	
Provision for depreciation of vehicles		180
Stock on hand on 31 May 1997	260	
Debtors	250	
Creditors		210
Sales		1,700
Cost of sales	960	
Rent and rates	60	
Insurance	80	
Wage and salaries	150	
Distribution costs	40	
Administration expenses	60	
Heat and light	10	
Printing postage and stationery	16	
Provision for bad debts		10
Interim dividend paid	25	
Bank		30
	3,310	3,310

Additional Information

1. Due to an error on the stock sheets, the value of the stock on hand on 31 May 1997 has been overstated by £30,000.
2. No record was made of goods purchased on credit for £40,000 on 30 May 1997 as the goods were not delivered until 2 June 1997.
3. Bad debts of £10,000 are to be written off and the provision for bad debts is to be adjusted to 5% of debtors.
4. The company rents showrooms at a cost of £6,000 per annum. The rent on these showrooms has been paid up to 31 July 1997.
5. In April 1997 the company paid rates of £12,000 for the half year to 30 September 1997.

6. In June 1996 the company sold an old vehicle for £1,000. This vehicle had originally cost £20,000 and had a book value at the date of sale of £4,000. The only entry made in the ledger in respect of this transaction was to debit the bank account and credit the vehicles account with the £1,000 received.
7. Depreciation is to be provided on the cost of fixed assets on hand at 31 May 1997 at the following annual rates.

    Land and buildings   2%
    Plant and machinery   10%
    Vehicles   20%

8. Provision is to be made for a final dividend of 10%.

You are required to prepare:

(a) the Trading and Profit and Loss Account and the Profit and Loss Appropriation Account of Candles Ltd for the year ended 31 May 1997; and
(b) the Balance Sheet as at that date.

(Suggested Solution on Page 158)

Question 10.7

The following trial balance was extracted from the ledger of Brackets Ltd. as at 30 June 1997.

	Debit £'000	Credit £'000
Ordinary share capital (£1 shares).....................................		750
Profit and loss account at 1 July 1996............................		338
10% debentures 2003..		100
Land and buildings at cost...	900	
Provision for depreciation of land and buildings..............		200
Plant and machinery at cost..	800	
Provision for depreciation of plant and machinery...........		400
Vehicles at cost	500	
Provision for depreciation of vehicles.............................		320
Stock on hand on 30 June 1997.....................................	400	
Debtors...	380	
Creditors		340
Sales...		2,570
Cost of sales	1,440	
Rent and rates	90	
Insurance...	120	
Wages and salaries	320	
Advertising and promotion	65	
Heat and light..	15	
Printing, postage and stationery.....................................	20	
Debenture interest		5
Provision for bad debts...		12
Interim dividend paid	40	
Bank		55
	5,090	5,090

Additional Information

1. Sales include £65,000 in respect of goods invoiced to a customer on 26 June 1997, on a sale or return basis. These goods were returned by the customer in July 1997. The cost of these goods, £50,000, was not included in the year-end stock figure.
2. Bad debts of £15,000 are to be written off and the provision for bad debts is to be adjusted to 5% of debtors.
3. Rent on the company's showrooms has been paid up to 31 July 1997. The cost of renting these showrooms is £12,000 per annum.

4. In April 1997, the company paid rates of £24,000 for the half year to 30 September 1997.
5. In July 1996, the company sold an old vehicle for £5,000. This vehicle had originally cost £20,000 and had a book value of £8,000 at the date of sale. The only entry made in the ledger in respect of this transaction was to debit the bank account and credit the sales account with the £5,000 received.
6. Sales staff are entitled to commission at the rate of 10% on the amount by which sales exceed £2 million.
7. No debenture interest was paid during the year.
8. Depreciation is to be provided on the cost of fixed assets on hand at 30 June 1997, at the following annual rates:
   Land and buildings   2%
   Plant and machinery   10%
   Vehicles   20%
9. Provision is to be made for a final dividend of 10%.

You are required to prepare:

(a) the Trading and Profit and Loss Account for the year ended 30 June 1997; and
(b) the Balance Sheet as at that date.

(Suggested Solution on Page 160)

Section 11

Manufacturing Accounts

Question 11.1

Manufacturers Ltd. is a small Irish company which produces automotive components for both the domestic and export markets. The following balances, as at the year-end date, have been extracted from the company's ledger.

Manufacturers Ltd.
Draft List of Selected Balances as at 31 December 1996

Purchases	£45,000
Carriage In	2,000
Direct Labour	26,000
Variable Factory Overheads	11,000
Fixed Factory Overheads	8,000
Rent and Rates	16,000
Light and Heat	4,000
Import Duty	4,500
Loose Tools Purchased	2,000
Plant and machinery at cost	30,000
Provision for depreciation of Plant and Machinery	12,000
Royalties on Manufacturing Processes	5,000
Hire of Special Equipment to Manufacture Complex Components	3,000
Quality Assurance Supervisor's Wages	12,000
Stocks on hand on 1 January 1996	
• Raw Materials	8,000
• Work in Progress	6,000
• Loose Tools	1,000

Additional Information

1. Depreciation is to be provided for 1996 on Plant and Machinery at the rate of 10% of original cost.
2. An additional £3,000, representing the direct factory wages for December 1996 as yet unpaid, should be accrued. Rent and Rates prepaid amount to £2,000.
3. Stocks on hand on 31 December 1996 were valued as follows:
   Raw Materials   £9,000
   Loose Tools   750
   Work in Progress   8,000
4. The 'Rent and Rates' and 'Light and Heat' expenses are to be apportioned 50:50 between Factory costs and Administrative expenses respectively.

Required

Prepare a Manufacturing Account for the company for 1996.

(Suggested Solution on Page 162)

Question 11.2

Mr. Murphy has been in business for some years as a manufacturer. The following balances, as at 31 December 1996, were extracted from his ledger.

	£ Debit	£ Credit
Purchases of Raw Materials.....................................	60,000	
Sales		150,000
Carriage Inwards	1,000	
Stock of Raw Materials on hand on 1 January 1996...	6,000	
Direct Manufacturing Wages	55,000	
Stock of Work-in-progress on hand on		
1 January 1996	7,000	
Debtors...	22,000	
Creditors...		17,000
Provision for Bad Debts		600
Bad Debts	400	
Machinery at cost	40,000	
Provision for depreciation of machinery....................		10,000
Rent of Premises..	12,000	
Capital..		28,000
Drawings...	1,500	
Stock of Finished Goods on hand on 1 January 1996 .	3,300	
Manufacturing Overheads.......................................	16,000	
Selling and Distribution Overheads..........................	11,000	
Bank...		39,600
Administration Overheads (non-manufacturing)	10,000	
	245,200	245,200

Additional Information

1. Stocks on hand at 31 December 1996 were valued as follows.
Raw materials	£ 8,000
Work-in-progress	5,000
Finished Goods	4,400
2. Depreciation is to be provided on machinery at the rate of 25% of cost.
3. The provision for bad debts is to be made equal to 10% of debtors.
4. £500 due for rent was not included in the ledger at the year-end. Rent of premises is to be apportioned 50% to manufacturing and 50% to selling and distribution overheads.

You are required to prepare for Mr. Murphy:

(a)   the Manufacturing, Trading and Profit and Loss Account, for 1996; and
(b)   the Balance Sheet as at 31 December 1996.

(Suggested Solution on Page 163)

Question 11.3

A client of your firm, Denis O'Connor, operates a manufacturing business. The following list of balances was extracted from his ledger at 31 December 1996:

	£ Debit	£ Credit
Sales		375,000
Purchases of raw materials	135,000	
Carriage inwards	3,000	
Direct wages	40,000	
Factory overheads	50,000	
Administrative overheads	35,000	
Selling and distribution overheads	45,000	
Rent and rates	14,000	
Bank interest and charges	2,000	
Bad debts written off for 1996	7,000	
Premises at cost	95,000	
Provision for depreciation on premises		19,000
Plant and equipment at cost	50,000	
Provision for depreciation on plant and equipment		18,000
Stock of raw materials on hand on 1 January 1996	37,000	
Stock of work-in-progress on hand on 1 January 1996	28,000	
Stock of finished goods on hand on 1 January 1996	8,000	
Debtors	76,000	
Provision for bad debts as at 31 December 1996		12,000
Prepayments	15,000	
Bank	38,000	
Creditors		56,000
Accruals		29,000
Capital at 1 January 1996		188,000
Drawings	19,000	
	697,000	697,000

Additional Information

1. The entire premises measures 10,000 square feet. The administration area amounts to 3,900 square feet. The sales and distribution area amounts to 1,500 square feet. The balance of 4,600 square feet is devoted exclusively to manufacturing. The rent and rates expense is to be apportioned in proportion to the area occupied.
2. Depreciation is to be provided for on premises at the rate of 2% per annum on the straight line basis, and on plant and equipment at the rate of 20% per annum on the reducing balance basis. All depreciation for the current year is to be included in 'Factory overheads'.
3. Stocks and work-in-progress on hand on 31 December 1996 were valued as follows:

Raw materials	£ 34,000
Finished goods	6,000
Work-in-progress	32,000

You are required to prepare:

(a) the Manufacturing Account and Trading and Profit and Loss Account for Denis O'Connor for 1996; and
(b) the Balance Sheet as at 31 December 1996;

(Suggested Solution on Page 165)

Question 11.4

The following Trial Balance was extracted from the ledger of Selkirk Ltd. for 1996:

	Debit £'000	Credit £'000
Stock of raw materials on hand on 1 January 1996	20	
Work-in-progress at 1 January 1996	7	
Stock of finished goods on hand on 1 January 1996	31	
Raw material purchases	250	
Carriage inwards	1	
Returns outwards		2
Wages	63	
Indirect production materials	2	
Royalties	3	
Salesmen's salaries and commission	9	
Heat and light	10	
Postage and telephone	2	
Rental of office space	12	
Office salaries	8	
General expenses	14	
Insurance	9	
Production plant and machinery	120	
Provision for depreciation of production plant and machinery		36
Office equipment at cost	50	
Provision for depreciation of office equipment		20
Delivery vans at cost	30	
Provision for depreciation of delivery vans		6
Sales		450
Sales returns	3	
Debtors and creditors	68	52
Ordinary share capital (£1 shares, fully paid)		100
Bank	12	
Provision for bad debts		2
Profit and Loss Account at 1 January 1996		56
	724	724

Additional Information

1. As a result of a stock-take carried out on 31 December 1996, stock has been valued as follows:
   Raw materials   £15,000
   Work-in-progress   9,000
   Finished goods   32,000
   Included in the finished goods stock is stock costing £4,000 which was damaged in a fire. This stock would realise only £2,000, if sold on the open market.

2. Wages included in the Trial Balance are to be split as follows:
   Direct wages   £40,000
   Indirect factory wages   23,000
                            63,000

3. Depreciation is to be provided at the following annual rates:
Production plant and machinery	10% on cost
Office equipment	20% on cost
Delivery vans	20% on net book value

4. Professional fees of £4,000 have not been provided for.

5. Rental of office space costs £8,000 per annum. Rent has been paid up to 30 June 1997.

6. Bad debts amounting to £1,200 should be written off. The provision for bad debts is to be adjusted to 5% of debtors.

7. Expenses are to be apportioned as follows:

	Production	*Administration*
Insurance	2/3	1/3
Heat and Light	3/4	1/4
General Expenses	1/2	1/2

You are required to prepare:

(a) the Manufacturing, Trading and Profit and Loss Account for 1996; and
(b) the Balance Sheet as at 31 December 1996.

(Suggested Solution on Page 167)

Question 11.5

Make-it Ltd. is a manufacturing company. The following balances appeared in its ledger on 30 September 1996.

Make-it Ltd.

Trial Balance as at 30 September 1996

	£	£
Advertising	39,960	
Audit Fee	7,875	
Bank	1,753,942	
Creditors		398,009
Debtors	167,400	
Direct Factory Wages	795,157	
Discount Given for Prompt Settlement	25,702	
Provision for Doubtful Debts		16,065
Factory General Expenses	11,925	
Factory Power	213,157	
Finished Goods Packaging and Delivery Expense ..	30,720	
Insurance	5,344	
Ordinary Share Capital		1,500,000
Light and Heat	20,880	
Office Furniture at Cost	120,750	
Office General Expenses	53,047	
Production Plant and Machinery at Cost	384,487	
Production Manager's Salary	23,437	
Profit and Loss Account as at 30 September 1995..		259,815
Provisions for depreciation to 30 September 1995:		
• Office Furniture		63,060
• Production Plant and Machinery		173,220
Office Salaries	69,457	
Purchases of Raw Materials	1,618,252	
Rent and Rates	28,080	
Repairs to Plant	11,827	
Sales		3,688,042
Sales Director's Salary	26,250	
Stocks on hand on 30 September 1995:		
• Finished Goods	450,697	
• Raw Materials	92,565	
• Work in Progress	147,300	
	6,098,211	6,098,211

Additional Information

1. Stocks on hand on 30 September 1996 were valued as follows:
   - Finished Goods   £541,365
   - Raw Materials   63,187
   - Work in Progress   137,220
2. Seven eighths of 'Rent and Rates', 'Light and Heat' and 'Insurance' are to be allocated to the factory. The figure for Insurance arises principally due to the cost of insuring property.
3. The provision for doubtful debts is to be adjusted to 5% of relevant debtors.
4. Depreciation is to be provided using the straight line method on plant and machinery at the rate of 25% per annum and on office furniture at the rate of 20% per annum.

Required

Based on the foregoing information, separately prepare a Manufacturing Account and a Trading and Profit and Loss Account for the year ended 30 September 1996, for presentation to the directors of Make-it Ltd, in as much detail as the information given permits.

(All calculations should be rounded to the nearest pound)

(Suggested Solution on Page 170)

Question 11.6

Tony Limited is a company which specialises in the manufacture of packing cases used for the despatch of goods in bulk.

At 31 December 1996 the following balances appeared in the company's ledger:

	£ Debit	£ Credit
Premises	370,000	
Plant and machinery	387,600	
Vehicles	79,700	
Provision for depreciation on premises		21,400
Provision for depreciation on plant and machinery		201,800
Provision for depreciation on vehicles		25,200
Purchases (net of returns) of Raw Materials	265,040	
Purchases (net of returns) of Packing cases (see note 4)	7,430	
Wages of Factory operatives	121,732	
Factory manager's salary	28,019	
Administrative wages and salaries	87,932	
Power heat and light	92,238	
Rates and Insurance	69,800	
Directors' fees	15,000	
Sales		876,863
Revenue reserves		10,030
Ordinary share capital (£1 shares)		100,000
8% Preference share capital (£1 shares)		50,000
7% Debentures 2001		500,000
Preference dividend paid	4,000	
Debenture Interest	35,000	
Stocks on hand on 1 January 1996:		
Raw materials	49,562	
Work-in-Progress	27,930	
Finished goods	61,070	
Packing cases (see Note 4)	987	
Trade debtors	62,731	
Discount allowed	1,462	
Trade creditors		28,540
Discount received		639
Bank	34,165	
Cash	13,074	
	1,814,472	1,814,472

Notes

1. Depreciation is to be provided for on fixed assets, using the methods and annual rates given below:

Premises	Straight line	2%
Plant and Machinery	Reducing balance	20%
Vehicles	Straight line	20%

2. Adjustment has not yet been made for:

Power, heat and light accrued	£3,462
Accrued wages and salaries – Factory operatives	1,569
Rates and Insurance Prepaid	10,600

3. Expenses should be apportioned as follows:

	Factory	Office
Rates and insurance	60%	40%
Power, heat and light	80%	20%
Depreciation of premises	60%	40%
Depreciation of plant and machinery	70%	30%

4. Occasionally, when production facilities are fully committed, Tony Limited has to buy in packing cases from another manufacturer to fulfil an urgent order.

5. Stocks on hand at 31 December 1996 were valued as follows:

Raw materials	£53,667
Work-in-progress	16,420
Finished goods	43,407
Packing cases	Nil

6. Corporation tax of £8,200 is to be provided for.

7. The directors have proposed an ordinary dividend of 20p per share.

Required

Prepare, for presentation to the directors of the company, a Manufacturing, Trading, Profit and Loss Account of Tony Limited for 1996 and a Balance Sheet as at 31 December 1996.

(Suggested Solution on Page 172)

Question 11.7

Manufacturing Company Ltd. is engaged in the manufacture and wholesale of automotive components. The following balances, as at 31 December 1996, have been extracted from the company's ledger.

Manufacturing Company Ltd.
Extract from the List of Balances as at 31 December 1996

Stocks on hand on 1 January 1996:	
Raw Materials	£17,000
Work in Progress	5,000
Finished Goods	6,000
Loose Tools	1,000
Finished Goods Packing Materials	500
Purchases of Raw Materials	48,000
Carriage In on Raw Materials	1,500
Direct Labour	38,000
Variable Factory Overheads	12,500
Fixed Factory Overheads	19,000
Rent and Rates	10,000
Light and Heat	14,000
Purchase of Finished Goods Packing Materials	2,500
10% Import Duty on Raw Materials	4,800
Loose Tools	3,000
Office Stationery	800
Salaries of Administrative Staff	19,000
Sales	226,400
Plant and machinery at cost	40,000
Provision for depreciation of plant and machinery	18,000
Manager's Company Car at cost	18,000
Provision for depreciation of Manager's Company Car	8,000
Car Running Expenses	3,500
Royalties on Manufacturing Processes	7,000
Hire of Special Equipment to Manufacture Complex Components	500
Factory Supervisor's Wages	12,000

Addtional Information

1. The 'Rent and Rates' and 'Light and Heat' expenses are to be apportioned as follows:
   Factory   75%;   Administration   25%
2. Depreciation for the year is to be provided at the following annual rates:
   Plant and Machinery   10% of Original Cost
   Manager's Company Car   20% using the Reducing Balance method
3. An additional £4,000, representing the direct factory wages for December 1996, as yet unpaid, should be accrued. Rent and Rates prepaid as at the year-end amount to £2,000.

4. Stocks on hand on 31 December 1996 were valued as follows:

Raw Materials	£10,000
Finished Goods	11,000
Finished Goods Packing Materials	1,200
Loose Tools	800
Work in Progress	8,000

Required

Prepare a Manufacturing Account for the company for 1996.

(Suggested Solution on Page 175)

Section 12

Final Accounts of Non-Profit Organisations

Question 12.1

The Slice Golf Club has two classes of membership – full members, who pay an annual subscription of £300, and associate members, who pay an annual subscription of £100.

On 1 January 1996 there were 200 full members, of whom 7 had paid their subscriptions for 1996 in advance, and 2 had still to pay their subscriptions for 1995. On the same date there were 100 associate members, of whom 3 had paid their subscriptions for 1996 in advance.

During 1996 the 2 full members who had not paid their subscriptions for 1995 were expelled from the club, while 12 new full members and 10 new associate members were admitted to the club.

During 1996 a total of £75,100 was received in respect of subscriptions. At 31 December 1996 there were no arrears of subscriptions outstanding in respect of 1996.

Required

Write up the Subscriptions Account for 1996.

(Suggested Solution on Page 176)

Question 12.2

The following summarised bank account was prepared for the Bunker Golf Club.

Bank

Receipts	£	Payments	£
Balance at 1 January 1996	1,200	Bar Suppliers	36,000
Subscriptions	14,900	Wages and Salaries	22,700
Bar Receipts	51,000	Course Repairs	3,000
Green Fees	3,000	Rates	2,600
Dance Receipts	700	Light and Heat	1,400
Competition Fees	2,500	Dance Expenses	500
		Competition Expenses	3,700
		Purchase of Mower	2,700
		Sundry Expenses	600
		Balance at 31 December 1996	100
	73,300		73,300

Additional Information

1.

	1 January 1996	*31 December 1996*
Bar Creditors	£ 5,000	£ 4,000
Bar Stock	7,000	8,000
Subscriptions in Arrears	400	700
Subscriptions in Advance	300	500
Light and Heat Due	100	200
Rates Prepaid	300	500

2. At 1 January 1996, the clubhouse and course were valued at £25,000, the fittings and furniture at £10,000 and the mowers and equipment at £5,500.
3. During 1996, an old mower with a book value of £500 at 1 January 1996, was traded in against a new mower, the list price of which was £3,000. £2,700 was paid to the supplier of the new mower.
4. Depreciation is to be provided for on fixed assets owned at the end of the year, on a straight line basis, at the following annual rates: Clubhouse and Course 2%, Fittings and Furniture 10%, Mowers and Equipment 20%.

You are required to prepare:

(a) the Income and Expenditure Account of the Bunker Golf Club for 1996; and

(b) the Balance Sheet of the club as at 31 December 1996.

(Suggested Solution on Page 177)

Question 12.3

The following is a summary of the South Yard Football Club's Bank Account for 1996.

Receipts	£	*Payments*	£
Bar Receipts	56,000	Balance at 1 January 1996	650
Members Subscriptions	7,400	Bar Suppliers	40,100
Members Tour Contributions	7,100	Bar Wages	2,200
Fund Raising for Tour	8,400	Light and Heat	2,400
		Telephone	650
		Insurance	6,400
		Tour Cost	17,500
		Buildings	7,500
Balance at 31 December 1996	3,900	Miscellaneous Expenses	5,400
	82,800		82,800

Additional Information

1. The assets of the club as at 1 January 1996 were valued as follows: Premises £30,000; Furniture and Equipment £8,500; Bar Stock £7,500 and Bar Suppliers were owed £3,100.
2. On 31 December 1996 Bar Stock was valued at £5,600 and suppliers were owed £2,900.
3. Furniture and Equipment is to be depreciated at the rate of 10% per annum on cost.
4. Insurance prepaid was as follows:
    31 December 1995   £1,400
    31 December 1996   £1,200
5. Subscriptions were received in advance as follows:
    31 December 1995   £750
    31 December 1996   £850
6. Light and Heat, Telephone, Insurance, Miscellaneous Expenses and Depreciation are to be apportioned equally between the bar and general activities.

You are required to prepare:

(a) a Bar Trading and Profit and Loss Account for 1996; and
(b) the Club's Income and Expenditure Account for 1996, and a Balance Sheet as at 31 December 1996.

(Suggested Solution on Page 180)

Question 12.4

You are the Treasurer of Crookstown Golf Club and have prepared the following receipts and payments account for 1996:

Receipts	£	£	Payments	£	£
Balance b/d: cash on hand		75	Balance b/d: bank account		1,200
Membership subscriptions:			Wages and salaries		
Ordinary members	11,000		Restaurant staff	3,800	
Associate members	1,600		Other staff	8,300	12,100
Life members	800	13,400	Restaurant purchases		8,600
Restaurant receipts		13,800	Rent and rates		1,600
Donations received		950	Light and heat		1,800
Deposit account		1,220	New computer		1,600
			Restaurant expenses		750
			Bank interest		240
			Deposit account		1,200
			Balance c/d:		
			Bank account	315	
			Cash on hand	40	355
		29,445			29,445

As Treasurer, you have been asked by the club's Management Committee to prepare additional financial statements (as set out in the requirement below) and you have been supplied with the following information:

Notes

1. The clubhouse should be valued at £18,000 at 31 December 1995, and at 31 December 1996.
2. All club equipment was valued at £10,400 at 31 December 1995. Depreciation should be charged at the rate of 20% per annum on the book value of all equipment held at the club's year-end.

3. Other assets and liabilities of the club are as follows:

	31 December 1996	*31 December 1995*
Restaurant creditors	£ 1,400	£ 1,600
Subscriptions due	400	—
Rates prepaid	320	200
Light and heat unpaid (accrued)	310	250
Restaurant Stock	930	850

4. Life subscriptions received are credited to a life subscriptions fund and written off to income over a 10 year period commencing in the year of receipt. The life subscriptions fund account balance on 1 January 1996 was £900, being in respect of £1,000 of life subscriptions received during 1995.
5. All subscriptions received from ordinary and associate members during 1996 were for that year.
6. One half of the charges for rent and rates, and light and heat, are in respect of the restaurant.
7. £1,200 was placed on deposit during the year and withdrawn, with interest earned, before the year-end.

You are required to prepare:

(a) a Statement of Affairs (opening Balance Sheet) as at 31 December 1995;
(b) a Restaurant Trading and Profit and Loss Account for 1996;
(c) an Income and Expenditure Account for 1996; and
(d) a Balance Sheet as at 31 December 1996.

(Suggested Solution on Page 183)

Question 12.5

The following is the Receipts and Payments Account of the Greenogue Rugby Club for the year ended 30 June 1997.

Receipts	£	£	Payments	£	£
Balances b/d:			Light and heat		1,400
Bank account	1,100		Wages and Salaries:		
Cash on hand	150	1,250	Bar staff	4,200	
			Other staff	8,090	12,290
Membership Subscriptions			Rent and Rates		2,000
Ordinary members	10,600		Insurance		780
Associate members	1,200		Bar Purchases		8,400
Life members	600	12,400	Repairs to Clubhouse		630
			New Equipment		1,500
Annual Dinner Dance			New Computer		2,000
Sale of tickets	1,500		Bank Interest and Charges		320
Raffle	230	1,730	Bar Expenses		620
			Dance Expenses		400
Bar Receipts		14,200			
Balance c/d – bank		820	Balance c/d – cash on hand		60
		30,400			30,400

Additional Information

1. At 30 June 1996, and 30 June 1997, the clubhouse was valued at £15,000.
2. Club equipment had a net book value of £9,300 at 30 June 1996. Depreciation, on the reducing balance method, should be charged at the rate of 10% per annum on club equipment, including new equipment. The new computer is to be depreciated at the rate of 20% per annum on the straight line basis. A full year's depreciation is charged in the year of purchase on club equipment and the computer.
3. The figure for ordinary members subscriptions received is comprised of:

Subscriptions for the year ended 30 June 1997	£9,800
Subscriptions for the year ended 30 June 1998	800
	10,600

    The associate members' subscriptions received are all in respect of the year ended 30 June 1997.
4. The club introduced a life subscription membership scheme for the first time in the year ended 30 June 1997. The life subscriptions received are to be credited to a life subscriptions fund and written off to income over a 10 year period, commencing in the year of receipt.

5. Other assets and liabilities of the club at 30 June were as follows:

	1996	1997
Bar stock	£2,300	£2,600
Bar creditors	1,800	1,900
Rates prepaid	300	350
Insurance prepaid	400	350
Electricity bills unpaid (accrued)	250	320

You are required to prepare:

(a) a Statement of Affairs as at 30 June 1996;
(b) a Bar Trading Account for the year ended 30 June 1997;
(c) an Income and Expenditure Account for the year ended 30 June 1997; and
(d) a Balance Sheet as at that date.

(Suggested Solution on Page 186)

Section 13

Departmental Accounts

Question 13.1

Ned Ryan has been in business for many years as a hardware merchant. The business is comprised of two retail departments, one selling building materials and one selling electrical goods. The following trial balance was extracted from his ledger at 31 December 1996.

	£ Debit	£ Credit
Sales of Building Materials.......................................		300,000
Sales of Electrical Goods		200,000
Purchases of Building Materials..............................	170,000	
Purchases of Electrical Goods	95,000	
Wages	160,000	
Administration Costs..	12,300	
Selling and Distribution Expenses...........................	7,100	
Bank Charges...	600	
Premises at Cost..	80,000	
Plant and Equipment at Cost	30,000	
Provision for depreciation on Premises.....................		6,000
Provision for depreciation on Plant and Equipment ...		10,000
Stock of Building Materials on hand on		
1 January 1996	15,000	
Stock of Electrical Goods on hand on		
1 January 1996	20,000	
Debtors	20,000	
Prepayments	5,000	
Provision for Bad Debts		5,000
Creditors and Accruals		18,000
Bank		15,000
Capital		61,000
	615,000	615,000

Additional Information

1. Stocks on hand on 31 December 1996 were valued as follows:
   Building Materials   £35,000
   Electrical Equipment   £20,000
2. The provision for bad debts is to be made equal to 40% of debtors.
3. Depreciation is to be provided for at the following annual rates:
   Premises   2% on the straight line basis
   Plant and Equipment   20% on the reducing balance basis
4. Expenses are to be allocated to each department in accordance with its ratio of sales to total sales.

You are required to prepare:

(a) a Departmental Trading and Profit and Loss Account for 1996, using in each case separate columns for the building materials department, the electrical goods department and the total business; and

(b) the Balance Sheet for the total business as at 31 December 1996.

(Suggested Solution on Page 189)

Section 14

Preparation of Final Accounts from Incomplete Records

Question 14.1

William Brook is a sole trader. He has asked you to prepare accounts for his first year of business which ended on 31 December 1996, and has supplied you with the following information:

1. Summarised bank account for 1996:

Lodgements	£164,000	Payments to creditors	£65,000
		Administration costs	45,000
		Selling expenses	15,000
		Financial expenses	8,000
		Drawings	10,000
		Balance at 31 December 1996	21,000
	164,000		164,000

2. All money received from debtors was lodged.
3. Lodgements included £27,000 capital introduced on 1 January 1996.
4. Other assets and liabilities at 31 December 1996, comprised the following:

Stock	£ 8,000
Debtors	24,000
Amount due in respect of purchases	15,000

You are required to prepare:

(a) the Trading and Profit and Loss Account of William Brook for 1996; and
(b) the Balance Sheet as at 31 December 1996.

(Suggested Solution on Page 191)

Question 14.2

Mary Lambe owns a boutique. She does not maintain full accounting records but has supplied you with the following information in respect of 1996:

1. Summarised Bank Account:

Lodgements	£283,000	Balance at 1 January 1996	£2,000
Balance at 31 December 1996	24,000	Payments to Creditors	209,000
		Wages	40,000
		Business Expenses	36,000
		Purchase of Fixed Assets	20,000
	307,000		307,000

2. Mary lodges all of the money she receives, except for £1,000 per month, which she takes for her own use.
3. Wages include £8,000 which Mary paid to her mother who does not work in the business.
4. Assets and liabilities at 1 January and 31 December 1996 included the following:

	1 January 1996	*31 December 1996*
Fixed Assets at Cost	£100,000	£108,000
Stock	60,000	40,000
Debtors	50,000	55,000
Creditors	15,000	14,000
Accrued Expenses	1,000	2,000
Prepaid Expenses	2,000	1,000

You are required to prepare:

(a) a Trading and Profit and Loss Account for Mary Lambe for 1996; and
(b) a Balance Sheet as at 31 December 1996.

(Suggested Solution on Page 193)

Question 14.3

Terry White, a sole trader, has provided you with the following information from his records for 1996:

	1 January 1996	*31 December 1996*
Stock	£ 22,000	£ 28,000
Debtors	18,000	26,000
Creditors	20,000	16,000
Bank	2,000	Unknown

He had the following transactions during the year to 31 December 1996:

Amounts Received from Debtors	£120,000
Amounts Paid to Creditors	80,000
Wages Paid	12,000
Expenses Paid	10,000
Drawings	13,000

Required

(a) prepare the Trading and Profit and Loss Account for Terry White for 1996; and

(b) prepare the Balance Sheet as at 31 December 1996.

(Suggested Solution on Page 195)

Question 14.4

John Blank owns a confectionery shop. Turnover is comprised solely of cash sales. In January 1997 the manager of the shop suddenly disappeared and John, alarmed by this, and by a serious decline in the business' bank balance, asked you to conduct an investigation.

You obtained the following information:

1. During the first half of 1996 the gross profit margin earned by the shop was 33 1/3%. The rate of VAT during this period was 15%.
2. From 1 July 1996 the gross profit margin was reduced to 25% and the rate of VAT was reduced to 10%.
3. The quantity of goods sold in the second half of 1996 was 50% higher than in the first half.
4. Purchases for the year (excluding recoverable VAT) amounted to £520,000.
5. Stocks, valued at cost, were as follows:
1 January 1996	£ 60,000
31 December 1996	80,000
6. Lodgements in respect of sales amounted to £635,000.

Required

Calculate the amount of any cash deficiency.

(Suggested Solution on Page 196)

Question 14.5

William Greene, a butcher, commenced in business on 1 January 1996, and completed his first year's trading on 31 December 1996. He has presented you with the following summaries:

Cheque Payment Summary		*Bank Lodgement Summary*	
Purchases	£130,000	Sales	
		(net of cash withdrawn)	£200,000
Light and heat	8,950	Capital introduced	30,000
Print, packaging and		Refunds from creditors	3,000
stationery	17,860		
Motor expenses	18,940		
Wages, PAYE and PRSI	15,400		
Rent	15,000		
Insurance	9,000		
	215,150		233,000

He has also explained that each month he withdrew £4,500 cash from the business which he spent as follows:

Wages	£2,800
Drawings	400
Cash purchases	1,100
Motor expenses	200
	4,500

Additional Information

1. Stock on hand on 31 December 1996 was valued at £12,000.
2. Direct debits for bank charges not shown in the Cheque Payment Summary amount to £2,800.
3. Light and heat includes a refundable deposit of £2,500 which will be repaid if he remains in business for two years.
4. Motor expenses includes his personal motor and travel expenses which amount to 20% of the total motor expenses.
5. Stationery and packaging materials on hand on 31 December 1996 were valued at £1,920.
6. The wages paid comprises the net wages for the year and PAYE and PRSI for the 11 months to 30 November 1996. The PAYE and PRSI due for the month ended 31 December 1996, amounts to £1,400.
7. Rent has been paid for 3 months in advance.
8. Insurance is paid 3 months in arrears.

You are required to prepare:

(a) the Trading and Profit and Loss Account for William Greene for 1996; and
(b) the Balance Sheet as at 31 December 1996.

(Suggested Solution on Page 197)

Question 14.6

George Martin is a sole trader whose financial year-end is 31 December. The following balances were extracted from his ledger:

	31 December 1996	*31 December 1995*
Stock	£30,000	£26,000
Debtors	36,000	42,000
Prepayments (light and heat)	15,000	10,000
Trade creditors	50,000	48,000
Accruals (office expenses)	19,000	20,000

Additional Information

1. Gross profit is at a mark-up of 25% on cost.
2. Fixed assets at 31 December 1995 were £60,000.
3. Capital at 31 December 1995 was £80,000.
4. Receipts from customers during 1996 totalled £350,000. All sales are made on credit.
5. Payments for 1996 were as follows:
    Light and Heat   £ 25,000
    Office Expenses   27,000
6. The proprietor's personal expenses for 1996 amounted to £13,500.
7. Bad debts of £4,000 were written off during 1996.
8. During 1996, discount received amounted to £6,000 while discount allowed amounted to £5,000.
9. Depreciation for 1996 amounted to £4,000.
10. The bank balance at 31 December 1995, was £10,000.

You are required to prepare:

(a) the Trading and Profit and Loss Account of George Martin for 1996; and
(b) the Balance Sheet as at 31 December 1996.

(Suggested Solution on Page 199)

Question 14.7

The following is a letter which you received from a friend of yours, Mr. B. Ward, who has not kept proper accounting records for his business.

Dear John,

Thank you for your kind offer to help me in organising my accounts. As you know, I won £10,000 in the Prize Bonds, which I received in December 1995, and decided to commence my own business as a contractor. On 2nd January 1996, I purchased a JCB digger, which I hope will last for 5 years, for £6,500.

Business was slow at first but picked up eventually. I kept a note of all work done and, on 31 December 1996, I had received cheques totalling £4,714 from various customers which had been lodged. This sum did not include work done just before Christmas, which I did not get a chance to invoice, and which amounted to £360.

I incurred very few expenses during the year except for repair bills. I added these up the other day and the cheque payments amounted to £572. Some other cheques which I wrote were in respect of insurance, £245, which coincided with the calendar year, and £416 in respect of petrol and diesel oil. The bank charged me £95 interest as I had a small overdraft during the year.

The debit balance per my bank statement on 31 December 1996 was £2,498 but I noticed that a cheque for £200 had not yet been presented.

I wrote a few other non-business cheques during the year. I do not know for how much exactly as I did not fill in the cheque stubs properly. Best to say that if there is any money missing then it should be charged by way of drawings.

I hope from what I have said that you can prepare some sort of accounts for me. Don't forget to provide for your own accountancy fee of £100.

Yours sincerely,

Brian Ward.

Required

(a)   prepare a Profit and Loss Account for 1996; and
(b)   prepare a Balance Sheet as at 31 December 1996.

(Suggested Solution on Page 201)

Question 14.8

Set out below is a letter you received recently from a friend, Joe Singleton.

31 January 1997

Dear Pat,

I would appreciate your help with my accounts. On 1 January 1996 I started a business as a retail stationer. To open a business bank account, I lodged the £12,000 redundancy payment cheque which I had received. The following were all my transactions for the year.

(1)	Total purchases on credit	£30,000
(2)	Total payments to creditors for purchases	27,000
(3)	Total sales on credit	50,000
(4)	Total receipts from debtors	48,000
(5)	Payments for expenses and rent	20,000
(6)	Drawings for my own use	6,000

Stock on hand on 31 December 1996 amounted to £4,000. All receipts and payments were put through the bank account.

I look forward to receiving your reply at your earliest convenience.

Yours sincerely,

Joe Singleton.

You are required to:

(a) prepare for Joe Singleton,
    (i)   the bank account for 1996;
    (ii) the Trading and Profit and Loss account for 1996;
    (iii) the Balance Sheet as at 31 December 1996; and
(b) list the reasons why the balance per the bank account in Joe Singleton's accounting records might be different from the bank balance, according to the Bank Statement at the same date.

(Suggested Solution on Page 203)

Question 14.9

The entire stock of Folders Ltd., whose financial year ends on 31 December, was destroyed by fire on 25 April 1997. The company requires an estimate of the cost of the stock destroyed in order to make a claim against its insurance company. It supplies you with the following information.

1. Purchases of goods for re-sale amounted to £296,750 in 1996, and to £102,250 in the period 1 January to 25 April 1997.
2. Sales, as shown in the Sales Journal, amounted to £376,000 in 1996, and to £127,300 in the period 1 January to 25 April 1997.
3. The rate of gross profit is approximately the same in each year.
4. The cost of the stock on hand on 31 December 1995 was £94,500 and on 31 December 1996 was £106,600.
5. Goods costing £2,650 were misappropriated by an employee in February 1996. The same employee admitted to misappropriating £500 from cash sales in January 1997.

Required

Estimate the cost of the stock destroyed in the fire.

(Suggested Solution on Page 205)

Question 14.10

Mr. Patterson is trading as a retail merchant selling two categories of goods as follows:

	Category A	Category B
Percentage Mark-up on Cost	25%	$33\frac{1}{3}\%$

On 11 August 1997 a fire destroyed his entire stock. The following information has been extracted from the accounting records:

1.

	1 January 1997	*11 August 1997*
Trade Debtors (gross)	£ 8,027	£ 11,000
Provision for Bad Debts	1,000	2,000
Trade Creditors	6,492	4,925
Stock on Hand		
– Category A	16,843	Unknown
– Category B	8,106	Unknown
Cash on Hand	900	1,200

2. Cash movements during the period from 1 January 1997 to 11 August 1997 were as follows:

Cheque payments for purchases for re-sale	£59,126
Cash received from debtors and subsequently lodged	83,555
Cash payments to trade creditors in respect of goods for re-sale	1,800

3. Bad debts amounting to £760 were written off and bad debts recovered amounting to £48 were received and immediately lodged during the period. In addition, discount allowed amounted to £612 and discount received amounted to £641.

The mix of purchases and sales consists of:
    Category A   70%
    Category B   30%

You are required to:

(a) reconstruct the cash account, and debtors and creditors control accounts, for the period 1 January to 11 August; and
(b) compute the cost of goods destroyed by the fire on 11 August.

(Suggested Solution on Page 205)

Question 14.11

Alan Strong, a sole trader, has asked you to prepare the accounts for his business for 1996, and has provided you with the following information:

Summarised Bank Account for 1996

Lodgements				Balance at 1 January 1996	£2,016
	(5)	£84,000		Payments to Creditors	42,900
				Wages and Salaries	8,100
				Rent and Rates	1,250
				Light and Heat	3,200
				Printing and Stationery	2,300
				Telephone	1,100
				Transfer to Deposit A/c (3)	5,000
				Purchase of Van (4)	6,500
				General Expenses	4,300
				Balance at 31 December 1996	7,334
		84,000			84,000

Additional Information

1. Details of other assets and liabilities are as follows:

	At 1 January 1996	At 31 December 1996
Stock at Cost	£ 6,300	£ 8,400
Debtors	4,100	4,600
Creditors	3,900	4,200
Wages and Salaries Due	500	750
Rates Due	200	300
Light and Heat Prepaid	400	300

2. The business owns a premises which was valued at £25,000 on 1 January 1996, and is to be valued at £22,500 on 31 December 1996.
3. £5,000 deposited in a bank deposit account during the year had earned interest of £400 by 31 December 1996. This interest is outstanding at 31 December 1996.
4. The new van is to be depreciated by 10% of cost in respect of 1996.
5. The following amounts were paid in cash, out of the money received from sales, before those receipts were lodged:

    £800   paid in general expenses
    £1,000 paid to creditors
    £3,600 withdrawn by the owner to cover personal expenses.

Required

(a) prepare a Statement of Affairs (opening Balance Sheet) for Alan Strong as at 1 January 1996;

(b) prepare a Trading and Profit and Loss Account for 1996; and

(c) prepare a Balance Sheet as at 31 December 1996.

(Suggested Solution on Page 207)

Question 14.12

On 1 September 1996 John Wells commenced trading as a wholesaler of ladies and gents' fashion garments. On 28 March 1997 his premises were engulfed in a fire in which all accounting records, cash on hand, stock and office equipment therein, were destroyed.

From duplicate records and other information supplied to you, you have been able to assemble the information set out in Schedules 1 to 4 inclusive.

Schedule 1 – Analysis of Bank Statements

Payments		Receipts	
Drawings	£7,420	Government Training Grants	£1,800
Trade Creditors	95,600	Cash Introduced	12,000
Wages	21,425	Receipts from Trade Debtors	125,500
PAYE taxation	3,750	Cash Sales	17,481
Expense Creditors	1,800	Long-term Loan	30,000
Cash Expenses (see Schedule 2)	4,080		186,781
Office Equipment	7,500		
Transit Van	22,000		
Loan Repayments	5,000		
Rent	2,400		
	170,975		

Schedule 2 – *Analysis of Cash Expenses*		*Schedule 3 –* *Balances as at 28 March 1997*	
Drawings	£980	Trade Creditors	£10,090
Wages	350	Expense Creditors	120
Expenses	450	Wages due	2,250
Purchases	2,300	PAYE due	625
	4,080	Trade Debtors	11,500

Schedule 4 – Other Information

1. A customer's balance of £2,760 had been set off against a balance due to him for goods supplied.
2. Bad debts written off amounted to £804 in the period.
3. Discount of £2,405 had been allowed to customers for early settlement of their accounts.
4. The insurance company has agreed to pay the following claims submitted in respect of the fire.

Stock	£7,800
Office equipment	6,800
Cash	160

5. Neither the transit van or the stock in it were damaged in the fire. This stock was valued at £4,500.
6. Depreciation is to be charged on the cost of the transit van at the rate of 20% per annum, or part thereof.
7. The rent charged to the business is £4,800 per annum.
8. The government grants were received in respect of staff training.

Required

Prepare for John Wells; a Profit and Loss Account for the period 1 September 1996 to 28 March 1997, and a Balance Sheet as at 28 March 1997.

N.B. *Ignore any interest chargeable on the loan.*
Ignore any VAT implications in the details supplied.

(Suggested Solution on Page 210)

Question 14.13

Ben Lewis is a sole trader, who carries on a cabinet manufacturing business. He does not have an accountant and he himself does not have any experience in maintaining proper accounting records. Accordingly, he has sought your assistance, as he wishes to extract accounts for the year ended 31 March 1997. From information supplied by Mr. Lewis and from your own investigations, you ascertain the following.

1. The Trial Balance at 1 April 1996 was as follows.

	£ Debit	£ Credit
Premises	40,000	
Provision for depreciation on premises		2,000
Plant	18,000	
Provision for depreciation on plant		4,500
Stock	16,000	
Debtors	14,000	
Bank	3,000	
Cash	500	
Creditors		18,000
Provision for legal claim		5,000
Capital		62,000
	91,500	91,500

2. An analysis of the bank lodgement dockets for the year revealed the following receipts.

Disposal of Old Machine as Scrap	£2,000
Receipts from Debtors	64,000
Cash Lodgements	27,000
Insurance Proceeds [See (6) below]	5,000
Inheritance from Uncle	12,000
	110,000

3. An analysis of the cheque stubs for the year revealed the following payments.

Payments to Suppliers	£58,000
New Machine	14,000
Wages and Expenses	11,100
Legal Claim [See (7) below]	6,400
Cash	5,700
Drawings	13,400
	108,600

4. The cash balance at 31 March 1997 was £400. During the year £9,400 in wages and expenses were paid out of cash.
5. All purchases were made on credit and all receipts from credit sales were lodged intact to the bank. Receipts from cash sales were occasionally used to pay cash expenses [see (4) above].
6. On 1 April 1996, Mr. Lewis had two machines. These had been bought for £9,000 each, 12 months previously, when he commenced business. During the year one of the machines was damaged by fire and had to be replaced. The insurance proceeds relate to the damaged machine which was ultimately disposed of.

7. On 31 March 1996, there was a legal claim pending against the business arising from the supply of defective cabinets. The amount paid out during the year was the final settlement of this claim (including legal fees).

8. When you reconciled the bank account, you noted that the bank had dishonoured a cheque for £3,000 from a customer. This had not been noted anywhere in Mr. Lewis' accounting records. According to Mr. Lewis, this balance should be written off as a bad debt. There were no other bad debts during the year.

9. Discounts of £1,200 and £2,100 were allowed and received respectively. On 31 March 1997, debtors owed £15,700, creditors were owed £16,100 and stock on hand was valued at £18,400.

10. Depreciation is to be provided using the straight line method, on premises at the rate of 5% per annum, and on plant at the rate of 25% per annum. A full year's depreciation is charged in the year of acquisition and none is charged in the year of disposal.

Required

Prepare for Mr. Lewis a Profit and Loss Account for the year ended 31 March 1997, and a Balance Sheet as at that date.

(Suggested Solution on Page 213)

Section 15

Ratio Analysis

Question 15.1

Outline some of the more important limitations of ratio analysis as a financial analysis technique.

(Suggested Solution on Page 216)

Question 15.2

Explain the purpose, and indicate the method of calculation, of each of the following ratios:

(a) Return on Capital Employed;
(b) Net Profit Margin;
(c) Stock Turnover;
(d) Current Ratio;
(e) Acid-Test Ratio; and
(f) Average Collection Period for Debtors.

(Suggested Solution on Page 217)

Question 15.3

The following information has been extracted from the accounting records of Jones Ltd. for 1996:

Extract from the Profit and Loss Account

Sales	£150,000
Purchases	100,000
Stock on hand on 1 January 1996	30,000
Stock on hand on 31 December 1996	50,000

Extract from the Balance Sheet

Fixed Assets	£170,000
Bank	6,000
Debtors	25,000
Stock	50,000
Creditors	30,000
Accruals	10,000
Short-term Bank Loan	14,000

Required

(a) calculate the following ratios for Jones Ltd.:
    (i) stock turnover;
    (ii) current ratio;
    (iii) acid-test ratio; and
(b) explain briefly the significance of any one of the above ratios.

(Suggested Solution on Page 218)

Question 15.4

Balance Sheets of J. Giles are as follows:

	31 March 1995		31 March 1996	
Fixed Assets		£260,000		£205,000
Current Assets				
Stock	£86,000		£84,000	
Debtors	94,000		58,000	
	180,000		142,000	
Current Liabilities				
Creditors	174,000	6,000	59,000	83,000
		266,000		288,000
Financed By:				
Capital at the start of the year		262,900		266,000
Net Profit for the year		15,600		36,000
Drawings during the year		−12,500		−14,000
		266,000		288,000

The following information was extracted from the Trading Accounts for the years ended 31 March 1995 and 1996 respectively:

Sales	£505,000	£385,000
Gross Profit	152,900	172,750
Opening Stock	82,000	86,000

Required

Calculate the following ratios for each year and comment on the position shown for the second year as compared to the first:

1. Gross Profit Margin;
2. Stock Turnover;
3. Current Ratio;
4. Acid-test Ratio; and
5. Period of Credit Given.

(Suggested Solution on Page 219)

Question 15.5

The following figures have been extracted from the trading and profit and loss account, and balance sheet, of Ted Sharp.

Extracts from the Trading and Profit and Loss Account
for the Year Ended 31 December 1996

Sales		£400,000
Cost of Sales		
Opening Stock	£80,000	
Purchases	310,000	
	390,000	
Closing Stock	120,000	270,000
Gross Profit		130,000
Expenses		
Selling Expenses..	32,000	
Entertainment Expenses...	41,000	
Administration Expenses	23,000	
Financial Expenses...	9,000	
Depreciation...	4,000	109,000
Net Profit		21,000

Extracts from the Balance Sheet as at 31 December 1996

Fixed Assets		
Cost..		£80,000
Provision for depreciation......................................		−15,000
		65,000
Current Assets		
Stock	£120,000	
Debtors...	55,000	
Bank..	38,000	
	213,000	
Current Liabilities		
Creditors...	48,000	165,000
Net Assets		230,000

Note: All sales are on credit.

You are required to:

(a) calculate each of the following ratios:
   (i)   Current ratio;
   (ii) Acid-test ratio;
   (iii) Stock turnover;
   (iv) Period of Credit Given to Debtors; and
(b) comment briefly on any one of the above ratios.

(Suggested Solution on Page 220)

Question 15.6

Balance Sheets of James Parker are as follows:

	31 March 1996		31 March 1997	
Fixed Assets		£85,300		£131,300
Current Assets				
Stock	£54,500		£79,500	
Debtors	55,200		80,700	
	109,700		160,200	
Current Liabilities				
Creditors	55,000	54,700	160,000	200
		140,000		131,500
Financed By:				
Capital at the start of the year		126,000		140,000
Net Profit for the year		24,000		4,000
Drawings during the year		−10,000		−12,500
		140,000		131,500

The following information was extracted from the Trading Accounts for the years ended 31 March 1996 and 1997 respectively:

Sales	£350,000	£460,000
Gross Profit	122,500	92,000
Opening Stock	52,500	54,500

Required

Calculate the following ratios for each year and comment on the position shown for the second year as compared to the first:

(a)   Gross Profit Margin;
(b)   Stock Turnover;
(c)   Current Ratio;
(d)   Acid-Test Ratio; and
(e)   Period of Credit Given.

(Suggested Solution on Page 221)

Question 15.7

The following are the management accounts of Appliances Ltd., a retail electrical business, for 1996:

Trading and Profit and Loss Account for the Year Ended 31 December 1996

	Small Electrical Goods		Large Electrical Goods		Total	
Sales		£30,000		£70,000		£100,000
Cost of Sales						
Opening Stock	£4,000		£10,000		£14,000	
Purchases	24,000		60,000		84,000	
	28,000		70,000		98,000	
Closing Stock	6,000	22,000	8,000	62,000	14,000	84,000
Gross Profit		8,000		8,000		16,000
Expenses						12,000
Net Profit						4,000

Balance Sheet as at 31 December 1996

Tangible Fixed Assets	Cost	Provision for Depreciation	Net Book Value
Leasehold Property	£80,000	£16,000	£64,000
Vehicles	24,000	12,000	12,000
Furniture and Fittings	8,000	2,000	6,000
	112,000	30,000	82,000
Current Assets			
Stock		14,000	
Debtors		18,000	
		32,000	
Current Liabilities			
Trade Creditors	12,000		
VAT payable	12,000		
Bank Overdraft	16,000	40,000	
Net Current Liabilities			−8,000
			74,000
Long-Term Liabilities			
Long-term Loan			−39,000
			35,000
Capital and Reserves			
Ordinary Share Capital			25,000
Revenue Reserves			10,000
			35,000

Required

(a) calculate the following ratios for 1996:
    (i)   Gross profit margin (separately for both small and large electrical goods);
    (ii) Stock turnover (separately for both small and large electrical goods);
    (iii) Current ratio;
    (iv) Acid-test ratio;
    (v)   Debtors days outstanding; and
    (vi) Creditors days outstanding.
(b) comment on the financial position of Appliances Ltd. in terms of both immediate liquidity and long-term liquidity; and
(c) make suggestions as to how Appliances Ltd. might improve its present financial position.

(Suggested Solution on Page 222)

Question 15.8

The following are the summarised final accounts of two similar manufacturing companies, Soda Ltd. and Tonic Ltd., for the year ended 31 December 1996:

Summarised Profit and Loss Accounts for the Year Ended 31 December 1996

	Soda Ltd.		Tonic Ltd.	
	£'000	£'000	£'000	£'000
Sales		700		540
Cost of Sales		310		230
Gross Profit		390		310
Debenture Interest	40		20	
Other Expenses	190	230	140	160
Net Profit		160		150

Balance Sheets as at 31 December 1996

	Soda Ltd.		Tonic Ltd.	
	£'000	£'000	£'000	£'000
Fixed Assets at cost		820		370
Provision for depreciation		360		80
		460		290
Current Assets				
Trade Debtors	115		60	
Stock	80		40	
Bank	10		–	
	205		100	
Current Liabilities				
Trade Creditors	80		55	
Net Current Assets		125		45
		585		335
Financed by:				
Shareholders' Funds		345		220
Debentures 2001		240		115
		585		335

Additional Information

1. Approximately 90% of each company's sales are made on credit.
2. Each company's stock level remains approximately constant throughout the year.

Required

Write a report to the Managing Director of Soda Ltd., comparing the performance of his company with that of Tonic Ltd.

Your report should include reference to appropriate ratios, and any other information which you consider relevant.

(Suggested Solution on Page 224)

Question 15.9

Your employer's finance department has recently developed a computer model, to assist in the prediction of the profit and loss account and balance sheet, for the first year of trading. By entering the sales forecast, and the values of the various parameters, the model will print a summary profit and loss account and an outline balance sheet. The model parameters are as follows:

Gross profit as a percentage of sales	40%
Selling expenses as a percentage of sales	14%
Administration costs, excluding interest	£12,000
Interest rate on long-term debt	10%
Return on capital employed – being:	
(Profit before interest divided by closing capital employed)	20%
Ratio of long-term debt to equity	1 : 1
Ratio of fixed assets to net current assets	3 : 1
Current ratio	2 : 1

The first trial of the model has a sales value of £100,000. The only expense items to be considered are selling, administration and interest.

You are required to prepare, in as much detail as possible, a forecast:

(a) Profit Statement based on the above information using an initial sales value of £100,000; and

(b) Balance Sheet.

(Suggested Solution on Page 228)

Question 15.10

Puzzles Ltd. has been trading for several years. Its authorised share capital is comprised of 400,000 ordinary shares of £1 each. The information set out below relates to the year ended 31 March 1997.

1. Capital employed at the year-end, 31 March 1997, consisted of 'Fixed Assets' and 'Net Current Assets'. Net Current Assets consist of Current Assets less Current Liabilities.
2. The cost of fixed assets at 31 March 1997, was £600,000. The provision for depreciation, after charging depreciation for the year ended 31 March 1997, amounted to 40% of the cost of fixed assets.
3. The ratio of the net book value of Fixed Assets to Net Current Assets was 1.5:1.
4. Current Assets (stock, debtors and bank) were twice the value of Current Liabilities.
5. The ratio of sales for the year to year-end Capital Employed was 2:1.
6. The average mark-up on cost during the period was 33 1/3%.
7. Net profit for the year (gross profit less business expenses and depreciation) amounted to 10% of sales.
8. The depreciation charge for the year was 10% of the cost of Fixed Assets held.
9. The issued ordinary share capital was £280,000.
10. Stock turnover for the year was 3 times. (The value of stock at the beginning and end of the year was the same).
11. Debtors days outstanding at 31 March 1997, were 30 (assume 360 days in a year).
12. The difference between the net profit for the year, and the balance on the profit and loss account at the end of the year, is the balance on the profit and loss account at the start of the year.

Required

You are required to construct from the above information the Profit and Loss Account, and the Balance Sheet for Puzzles Ltd., for the year ended 31 March 1997, in as much detail as the information supplied permits.

(Suggested Solution on Page 229)

Question 15.11

One of your clients has provided you with the following extracts from his final accounts:

	1996	1995
Sales	£960,000	£720,000
Cost of Sales	576,000	360,000
Gross Profit	384,000	360,000

The Gross Profit Rate achieved in 1995 is the norm for the type of goods sold, and your client is concerned about the decrease in 1996 relative to 1995.

The following occurred during 1996:

1. Sales of a new line of goods amounted to £100,000. The Gross Profit margin on these sales is 35%. These goods were not affected by items (2) to (6) below.
2. Stock which had cost £20,000 became obsolete and was sold for £5,000.
3. Goods purchased for half price at a supplier's closing down sale cost £40,000. Half of these were sold prior to the year end.
4. Sales revenue from seasonal promotions totalled £60,000. All items sold during these promotions were sold at 75% of normal price.
5. Goods costing £30,000 had to be destroyed when they became damp.
6. In order to meet a large order it was necessary to buy some stock from a new supplier. These goods cost 20% more than normal and were sold for £50,000.

Required

Determine whether the above factors account for the fall in the Gross Profit Rate or whether further investigations are necessary.

(Suggested Solution on Page 231)

Part 2
Suggested Solutions

Section 1

The Trial Balance, Accounting Concepts, Capital and Revenue Expenditure

Suggested Solution to Question 1.1

1. Errors of Omission

When a transaction is not recorded at all, the Trial Balance will still balance. For example, if a business sold goods to Mr. Thomas for £100 but the transaction was not entered in either the sales account or Mr. Thomas' account, the Trial Balance would not show a difference between its two sides because an amount has not been entered on either the debit or the credit side. This involves an error of omission.

2. Errors of Commission

Errors of commission occur where the correct amount is entered in both the relevant classes of account, but in the wrong person's account. For example, if a sale of goods for £100 to K. Green was entered into the account of C. Green (also a debtor), the Trial Balance would still balance.

3. Errors of Principle

Where an item is entered in the wrong class of account the Trial Balance still balances. For example, if a fixed asset purchase is debited to an expense account in error this is an error of principle.

4. Compensating Errors

Compensating errors occur where errors cancel each other out but the Trial Balance totals are still equal. For example, if the sales account was added up to be £100 too much and the purchases account was added up to be £100 too much, then these two errors would cancel out in the Trial Balance (i.e. the totals of both the Debit and Credit sides would be £100 too much).

5. Errors of Original Entry

Where an original figure is incorrect, yet double-entry rules are correctly observed using this incorrect figure, the Trial Balance will not show a difference.

For example, if goods worth £150 are sold, but an error is made in the invoice so that sales are incorrectly credited with £130 and the personal debtor account is also debited with £130, the Trial Balance will not reveal the error.

6. Complete Reversal of Entries

Where the correct amounts are used but each item is shown on the wrong side of the account, the Trial Balance will balance. For example, if a cheque for £200 is issued to D. Barker (a creditor) and the entry made is to Debit Bank £200 and Credit D. Barker £200, the Trial Balance would not highlight the fact that the debit and credit entries were mixed up.

Suggested Solution to Question 1.2

Fundamental Accounting Concepts are defined in SSAP 2 as 'the broad basic assumptions which underlie the periodic financial accounts of business enterprises'.

Suggested Solution to Question 1.3

1. The Going Concern Concept

The going concern concept means that when preparing the accounts of an entity, it is assumed that the entity will continue in operational existence for the foreseeable future. This means in particular that the profit and loss account and the balance sheet are prepared on the assumption that there is no intention, or necessity, to liquidate or curtail significantly the scale of operation.

2. The Accruals Concept

The accruals concept means that revenue and costs are accrued (that is, recognised as they are earned or incurred, not as money is received, or paid), matched with one another so far as their relationship can be established or justifiably assumed, and dealt with in the Profit and Loss Account, of the period to which they relate, provided that where the accruals concept is inconsistent with the 'prudence' concept, the prudence concept prevails. The accruals concept implies that the profit and loss account reflects changes in the amount of net assets that arise as a result of the transactions of the relevant period (other than distributions or subscriptions of capital and unrealised surpluses arising on revaluation of fixed assets). Revenues and profits, dealt with in the profit and loss account, are matched with associated costs incurred in earning them (so far as those are material and identifiable), by including in the same account the costs incurred in earning them.

3. The Consistency Concept

The consistency concept means that there is consistency of accounting treatment of like items within each accounting period, and from one period to the next.

4. The Prudence Concept

The prudence concept means that revenue and profits are not anticipated, but are recognised by inclusion in the profit and loss account, only when realised in the form either of cash or of other assets, the ultimate cash realisation of which can be assessed with reasonable certainty, provision is made for all known liabilities (expenses and losses) whether the amount of these is known with certainty, or is a best estimate in the light of the information available.

The relative importance of these concepts will vary according to the circumstances of the particular case. The only provision for putting them in any order of priority in SSAP 2 is a requirement that, where the accruals concept is inconsistent with the prudence concept, the latter should prevail.

Suggested Solution to Question 1.4

Accounting bases are the methods developed for applying fundamental accounting concepts to financial transactions and items, for the purpose of financial accounts, and, in particular,

(a) for determining the accounting periods in which revenue and costs should be recognised in the profit and loss account; and
(b) for determining the amounts at which material items should be stated in the balance sheet.

Where a choice of acceptable accounting bases is available, judgement must be exercised in choosing those which are appropriate to the circumstances and are best suited to present fairly the concern's results and financial position, the bases thus adopted then become the concern's accounting policies.

Suggested Solution to Question 1.5

Accounting policies are the specific accounting bases selected and consistently followed by a business enterprise as being, in the opinion of the management, appropriate to its circumstances and best suited to fairly present its results and financial position.

Suggested Solution to Question 1.6

In circumstances where more than one accounting basis is acceptable in principle, the accounting concern's reported results and financial position, and the view presented, can be properly appreciated only if the policies followed in dealing with material items are also explained. For this reason adequate disclosure of the accounting policies is essential to the fair presentation of financial accounts.

Suggested Solution to Question 1.7

Capital expenditure is expenditure incurred on the purchase or improvement of fixed assets. Capital expenditure will increase the value of the firm incurring the expenditure, by increasing the value of its fixed assets. Thus, capital expenditure will result in increased figures for the fixed asset category in the Balance Sheet. Expenditure incurred on the improvement of fixed assets refers to costs which are necessarily incurred to make those fixed assets operational, for example, delivery costs, installation costs, legal fees etc.

Suggested Solution to Question 1.8

Revenue expenditure, on the other hand, is expenditure incurred on a day-to-day basis to continue the operations of the business. These costs will not increase or enhance the value of a fixed asset, and therefore should be charged directly to the Profit and Loss Account as incurred.

Suggested Solution to Question 1.9

The distinction between Revenue expenditure and Capital expenditure is extremely important as, if expenditure is incorrectly treated in the accounts, either that capital expenditure is incorrectly treated as revenue expenditure, or vice versa, then both the Balance Sheet figures and the Profit and Loss Account figures will be incorrect. For example, if a capital cost, say the delivery cost of a new machine, is treated as revenue expenditure, then the expenses in the Profit and Loss Account will be overstated by that amount (and thus profit understated by that amount), and fixed assets will also be understated by the same amount.

Section 2

Depreciation

Suggested Solution to Question 2.1

Depreciation is a measure of the wearing out, consumption or other reduction in the useful economic life of a fixed asset, whether arising from use, the passage of time or obsolescence through technological or market changes. As it is a consequence of carrying out the normal operations of a business, it is charged as an expense in the Profit and Loss Account. Depreciation should be allocated so as to charge a fair proportion of the cost, or valuation of a fixed asset, to each accounting period expected to benefit from its use. In practice this involves subjective judgement, so the estimated useful lives of assets (and therefore the charge for depreciation in the accounts) should be reviewed regularly and when necessary, revised.

The causes of this diminution in value (depreciation) include:

- physical deterioration (eg. wear and tear, erosion or decay);
- economic factors such as obsolescence or inadequacy;
- time factors whether legal, natural or other;
- depletion of assets which are of a wasting nature owing to extraction of raw materials from them.

Suggested Solution to Question 2.2

The purpose of depreciation is to reflect in accounts the diminution in the value of most fixed assets as a result of use, the passage of time or obsolescence through technological or market changes (in accordance with the accruals concept), NOT to provide for the replacement of fixed assets, which it does not necessarily do. Since depreciation is a 'book entry' (i.e.. the creation of an expense in the Profit and Loss Account without any money leaving the business or being set aside within it), charging depreciation does not lead to a build-up of funds which could be used to replace assets at the end of their useful economic life. Assets can be replaced only if cash or loan finance is available and no amount of depreciation will generate either of these. In other cases, for example, with land or buildings, management may never, or only in the very long term, consider replacing the asset. Where there is no intention to replace an asset it is still depreciated. Thus, the depreciation charge does not represent a provision for future replacement.

Suggested Solution to Question 2.3

Prior to the issue of SSAP12 (in 1977), freehold and long leasehold properties were very rarely depreciated. It was contended that, as property values tended to rise instead of fall, it was inappropriate to charge depreciation. However, the collapsing property prices in the mid 1970's leading to the massive write-down of asset valuations in company accounts, caused the Accounting Standards Committee (ASC) to consider mandating depreciation provisions on all assets, with the exception of freehold land. In addition, at this time, the proliferation and inconsistency of accounting methods for depreciation was considered by the accounting profession to be incompatible with accounting conventions such as consistency and prudence.

Suggested Solution to Question 2.4

Buildings should be depreciated even if they are increasing in value for the following reasons:

- buildings have a finite, albeit long, useful economic life and they will eventually fall into disrepair and become obsolete;
- according to Statement of Standard Accounting Practice No. 12, it is not appropriate to omit charging for the depreciation of an asset on the grounds that its current Market Value is greater than its Net Book Value

Buildings may be revalued to show the increasing value in the accounts. In this case, the depreciation charge will be then based on the revalued amount, so an increased charge will become necessary.

Suggested Solution to Question 2.5

The cost of leasehold land should be depreciated over the life of the relevant lease, or, if this is unknown, over a base approximation of its life. Depreciation is warranted here because, as the leasehold is of a finite duration, its ultimate replacement should be provided for by way of an annual depreciation charge.

Freehold land however, should not normally be depreciated because it has an infinite useful economic life. Freehold land may have to be depreciated in the following circumstances:

- if the land is subject to depletion by, for example, the extraction of minerals;
- if its value is adversely affected by considerations such as a change in the desirability of its location.

Suggested Solution to Question 2.6

(a)   Plant (at Cost)

Jan 1	Balance b/d	194,000		Disposals of Plant	21,000
	Bank (Additions)	38,000	Dec 31	Balance c/d	211,000
		232,000			232,000

Vehicles (at Cost)

Jan 1	Balance b/d	58,000		Disposals	25,000
	Bank (Additions)	20,000	Dec 31	Balance c/d	53,000
		78,000			78,000

(b)   Provision for Depreciation on Plant

	Disposals of Plant[1]	8,400	Jan 1	Balance b/d	82,000
				Profit and Loss[3]	42,200
Dec 31	Balance c/d	115,800			
		124,200			124,200

Provision for Depreciation on Vehicles

	Disposals of Vehicles[2]	20,000	Jan 1	Balance b/d	30,000
Dec 31	Balance c/d	20,600		Profit and Loss[4]	10,600
		40,600			40,600

(c)   Disposals of Plant

	Plant at Cost	21,000	Provision for Depreciation	8,400
			Bank	8,000
			Profit and Loss (Loss)	4,600
		21,000		21,000

Disposals of Vehicles

	Vehicles at Cost	25,000	Provision for Depreciation	20,000
			Bank	7,200
	Profit and Loss (Profit)	2,200		
		27,200		27,200

[1] Calculation of Provision for Depreciation at Date of Disposal of Plant

Year	Value	Rate	Amount
1994	21,000	20%	4,200
1995	21,000	20%	4,200
1996	Nil		Nil
			8,400

[2] Calculation of Provision for Depreciation at Date of Disposal of Vehicles

Year	Value	Rate	Amount
1992	25,000	20%	5,000
1993	25,000	20%	5,000
1994	25,000	20%	5,000
1995	25,000	20%	5,000
1996	Nil		Nil
			20,000

[3] Depreciation on plant remaining after disposal: $[(£194,000 - £21,000) + £38,000] \times 20\%$ = £42,200

[4] Depreciation on vehicles remaining after disposal: $[(£58,000 - £25,000) + £20,000] \times 20\% = £10,600$

Suggested Solution to Question 2.7

(a)   Plant (at Cost)

1996		£	1996		£
June 1	Balance b/d	84,000	Dec 31	Disposal of Plant (W1)	25,000
1997			1997		
Jan 1	Bank (W2)	34,000	May 31	Balance c/d	93,000
		118,000			118,000

(b)   Provision for Depreciation of Plant

1996		£	*1996*		£
Dec 31	Disposal of Plant (W3)	12,808	June 1	Balance b/d	32,000
1997			*1997*		
May 31	Balance c/d	33,954	May 31	Profit and Loss (W4)	14,762
		46,762			46,762

(c)   (Profit and Loss on) Disposal of Plant

1996		£	*1996*			£
Dec 31	Plant (W1)	25,000	Dec 31	Prov. for Dep. of Plant (W3)		12,808
			Dec 31	Bank		10,000
			1997			
			May 31	Profit and Loss A/c (Loss)		2,192
		25,000				25,000

WORKINGS

W1   Cost of Plant Disposed of

Initial Cost		£16,000
Other Capitalised Costs		
Installation Cost	£1,000	
Transport Costs	3,000	
Additional Part	5,000	9,000
		25,000

The cost of repairs in August 1995 is revenue expenditure and is therefore not included above.

W2   Cost of New Machine

Initial Cost		£24,000
Other Capitalised Costs		
Installation Costs	£4,000	
Repairs to put the Machine into working order		
	6,000	10,000
		34,000

The cost of repairs has been capitalised as they 'added value' to the machine by putting it into working order.

W3   Depreciation on Machine Disposed of on 31 December 1996

		Value	Depreciation
Y/E 31 May 1993	Original Cost	16,000	
	Installation Charges	1,000	
	Transport Costs	3,000	
		20,000	
	Depreciation @ 20%	−4,000	4,000
		16,000	
Y/E 31 May 1994	Depreciation @ 20%	−3,200	3,200
		12,800	
Y/E 31 May 1995	Depreciation @ 20%	−2,560	2,560
		10,240	
Y/E 31 May 1996	New Part	5,000	
		15,240	
	Depreciation @ 20%	−3,048	3,048
		12,192	12,808

W4   Depreciation Charge for the Year Ended 31 May 1997

Cost Balance at 31 May 1997 (per Plant account)		£93,000
Provision for Depreciation at 31 May 1997:		
Opening Balance	£32,000	
Depreciation on Plant Disposed of	−12,808	−19,192
		73,808
Depreciation @ 20%		14,762

Suggested Solution to Question 2.8

(a)   Machinery (at Cost)

1995		£	1995		£
			Mar 31	Disposal of Machinery (W1)	36,000
Jan 1	Balance b/d	150,000	Dec 31	Balance c/d	114,000
		150,000			150,000
1996			1996		
Jan 1	Balance b/d	114,000	Sept 30	Disposal of Machinery (W1)	13,000
Dec 31	Purchases	13,000	Dec 31	Balance c/d	114,000
		127,000			127,000

(b)   Provision for Depreciation of Machinery

1995		£	1995		£
Mar 31	Disposal of Machinery (W2)	11,457	Jan 1	Balance b/d	30,000
Dec 31	Balance c/d	28,089	Dec 31	Profit and Loss (W3)	9,546
		39,546			39,546
1996			1996		
			Jan 1	Balance b/d	28,089
Dec 31	Balance c/d	36,680	Dec 31	Profit and Loss (W3)	8,591
		36,680			36,680

(c)   Disposal of Machinery

1995		£	1995		£
Dec 31	Machinery (W1)	36,000	Dec 31	Prov. for Dep. of Mach. (W2)	11,457
	Profit and Loss A/c			Bank	29,000
	(Profit)	4,457			
		40,457			40,457
1996			1996		
			Sept 30	Bank (£8,000 – £2,000)	6,000
Dec 31	Machinery (W1)	13,000		Profit and Loss A/c	
				(Loss)	7,000
		13,000			13,000

Workings

W1	Cost of Machines Disposed of	1995	1996
	Original Cost	24,000	10,000
	Installation Charges	4,000	2,000
	Transport Costs	2,000	1,000
	Additional Part	6,000	—
		36,000	13,000

The cost of repairs in April 1993 is revenue expenditure and therefore is not included above.

W2 Depreciation on Machine Disposed of in 1995

		Value	Depreciation
1991	Original Cost	24,000	
	Installation Charges	4,000	
	Transport Costs	2,000	
		30,000	
	Depreciation @ 10%	−3,000	3,000
		27,000	
1992	Depreciation @ 10%	−2,700	2,700
		24,300	
1993	New Part	6,000	
		30,300	
	Depreciation @ 10%	−3,030	3,030
		27,270	
1994	Depreciation @ 10%	−2,727	2,727
		24,543	11,457

W3 Depreciation Charge for 1995 and 1996

	Cost	Provision for Depreciation	Net	Charge
Balance at 1 January 1995	150,000	30,000	120,000	
Machine Sold in 1995 (W1/W2)	36,000	11,457	−24,543	
			95,457	
1995 Depreciation @ 10%			−9,546	9,546
Net Book Value at 31 December 1995			85,911	
1996 Depreciation @ 10%			−8,591	8,591
			77,320	

Note Depreciation was not charged in the above workings on the machine disposed of in 1996 as it was not held at any year-end.

Suggested Solution to Question 2.9

Machinery at Cost

1.7.93	Bank	10,000			
	Bank	15,000	30.6.94	Balance c/d	25,000
		25,000			25,000
1.7.94	Balance b/d	25,000	30.6.95	Disposal	15,000
30.6.95	Trade-In Allowance	6,000			
	Bank	18,000	30.6.95	Balance c/d	34,000
		49,000			49,000
1.7.95	Balance b/d	34,000	30.6.96	Balance c/d	34,000
1.7.96	Balance b/d	34,000	1.7.96	Disposal	34,000
1.7.96	Trade-In Allowance	15,000			
	Bank	10,000	30.6.97	Balance c/d	25,000
		59,000			59,000

Provision for Depreciation of Machinery

30.6.95	Disposal	*6,000	30.6.94	Profit and Loss	5,000
30.6.95	Balance c/d	4,000	30.6.94	Profit and Loss	5,000
		10,000			10,000
			1.7.95	Balance b/d	4,000
30.6.96	Balance c/d	10,800	30.6.96	Profit and Loss	6,800
		10,800			10,800
1.7.96	Disposal	10,800	1.7.96	Balance b/d	10,800
30.6.97	Balance c/d	5,000	30.6.97	Profit and Loss	5,000
		15,800			15,800

* 2 Years × 1/5 × £15,000 = £6,000

Machinery Disposals

			30.6.95	Provision for		
				Depreciation		6,000
				Trade-In Allowance		6,000
30.6.95	Machinery	15,000		Profit and Loss		3,000
		15,000				15,000
			1.7.96	Provision for		
				Depreciation		10,800
				Trade-In Allowance		15,000
1.7.96	Machinery	34,000		Profit and Loss		8,200
		34,000				34,000

Profit and Loss Account Extracts for the Years Ended 30 June

	1994	1995	1996	1997
Provision for Depreciation	5,000	5,000	6,800	5,000
Loss on Machinery Sold	—	3,000	—	8,200
	5,000	8,000	6,800	13,200

Balance Sheet (Extracts) as at 30 June

	1994	1995	1996	1997
Machinery at Cost	25,000	34,000	34,000	25,000
− Depreciation to Date	−5,000	−4,000	−10,800	−5,000
	20,000	30,000	23,200	20,000

Suggested Solution to Question 2.10

(a)   Premises at Cost

1 Jan	Balance b/d	200,000	31 Dec	Balance c/d	200,000

(b)   Plant and Equipment at Cost

1 Jan	Balance b/d	80,000	31 Dec	Balance c/d	80,000

(c)   Vehicles at Cost

1 Jan	Balance b/d	20,000		Disposal	20,000

(d) Provision for Depreciation of Premises

31 Dec	Balance c/d	16,000	1 Jan	Balance b/d	12,000
				Profit and Loss	4,000
		16,000			16,000

(e) Provision for Depreciation of Plant and Equipment

31 Dec	Balance c/d	39,040	1 Jan	Balance b/d	28,800
				Profit and Loss	10,240
		39,040			39,040

(f) Provision for Depreciation of Vehicles

	Disposal	4,000	1 Jan	Balance b/d	4,000

(g) Vehicle Disposals

			Provision for Depreciation	4,000
			Bank	12,000
	Vehicles at Cost	20,000	Loss on Disposal	4,000
		20,000		20,000

Depreciation Calculations

Premises

Year	Value		Rate		Amount
1993	£200,000	×	2%	=	£4,000
1994	200,000	×	2%	=	4,000
1995	200,000	×	2%	=	4,000
					12,000
1996	200,000	×	2%	=	4,000

Plant and Equipment

	Calculation		Value	Depreciation
1994	Cost		£80,000	
	Depreciation	*£80,000 @ 20%	−16,000	£16,000
			64,000	
1995	Depreciation	£64,000 @ 20%	−12,800	12,800
	At 1 January 1996		51,200	28,800
1996	Depreciation	£51,200 @ 20%	−10,240	10,240
			40,960	39,040

Vehicles

1995		*£20,000 @ 20%		£4,000
1996		**Nil		

* A full year's depreciation is provided in the year of purchase
** No depreciation is provided in the year of disposal

Suggested Solution to Question 2.11

The factors which should be considered in the assessment of depreciation and its allocation to accounting periods are:

(a) the amount at which the asset being depreciated is carried in the accounts;
(b) the length of assets' expected useful economic lives to the business of the enterprise, having due regard to the incidence of obsolescence; and
(c) the estimated residual value of assets at the end of their expected useful economic lives in the business of the enterprise.

Suggested Solution to Question 2.12

A change from one method of providing for depreciation to another is permissible only on the grounds that the new method will give a fairer presentation of the results, and of the financial position of the business.

Suggested Solution to Question 2.13

If at any time there is a permanent diminution in the value of an asset, and the net book value is considered not to be recoverable in full (perhaps as a result of obsolescence or a fall in demand for a product), the net book value should be written down immediately to the estimated recoverable amount, which should then be written off over the remaining useful economic life of the asset. If at any time the reasons for making such a provision cease to apply, the provision should be written back to the extent that it is no longer necessary.

Suggested Solution to Question 2.14

The charge for depreciation of revalued fixed assets should be based on the revalued amounts and the remaining useful economic lives. Depreciation charged prior to revaluation should not be written back to the Profit and Loss Account, except to the extent that it relates to a provision for permanent diminution in value which is subsequently found to be unnecessary.

Suggested Solution to Question 2.15

The disclosure requirements of SSAP 12 are:

(a) the following should be disclosed in the financial statements for each major class of depreciable asset:
     (i)   the depreciation method used;
     (ii) the useful economic lives or the depreciation rates used;
     (iii) total depreciation charged for the period; and
     (iv) the gross amount of depreciable assets and the related provision for depreciation;
(b) where there has been a change in the depreciation method used, the effect, if material, should be disclosed in the year of change. The reason for the change should also be disclosed; and
(c) where assets have been revalued the effect of the revaluation on the depreciation charge should, if material, be disclosed in the year of revaluation.

Section 3

Bad Debts and Provisions for Doubtful Debts

Suggested Solution to Question 3.1

(a)   Bad Debts

1994		£	1994		£
Dec 31	Debtors	12,500	Dec 31	Profit and Loss	12,500
1995			1995		
Dec 31	Debtors	8,200	Dec 31	Profit and Loss	8,200
1996			1996		
Dec 31	Debtors	8,000	Dec 31	Profit and Loss	8,000

(b)   Provision for Doubtful Debts

1994		£	1994		£
Dec 31	Profit and Loss	3,350	Jan 1	Balance b/d	8,750
Dec 31	Balance c/d	5,400			
		8,750			8,750
1995			1995		
Dec 31	Balance c/d		Jan 1	Balance b/d	5,400
	(2,000 + *7,320)	9,320			
			Dec 31	Profit and Loss	3,920
		9,320			9,320
(* see part 5)					
1996			1996		
Dec 31	Profit and Loss	580	Jan 1	Balance b/d	9,320
Dec 31	Balance c/d	8,740			
		9,320			9,320

(c)   Provision for Discount on Debtors

1994		£	1994		£
Dec 31	Balance c/d (see Part 5)	2,592	Dec 31	Profit and Loss	2,592
1995			1995		
Dec 31	Balance c/d	3,514	Jan 1	Balance b/d	2,592
			Dec 31	Profit and Loss	922
		3,514			3,514
1996			1996		
Dec 31	Balance c/d	4,195	Jan 1	Balance b/d	3,514
			Dec 31	Profit and Loss	681
		4,195			4,195

(d) <u>Profit and Loss Account Extracts for the Years Ended 31 December</u>

	1994	1995	1996
Bad Debts	£12,500 *Dr.*	£8,200 *Dr.*	£8,000 *Dr.*
Increase in Provision for Discount on Debtors	2,592 *Dr.*	922 *Dr.*	681 *Dr.*
In/Decrease in Provision for Doubtful Debts	3,350 *Cr.*	3,920 *Dr.*	580 *Cr.*

(e) <u>Balance Sheet Extracts as at 31 December</u>

	1994	1995	1996
Gross Debtors	£135,000	£190,000	£220,000
Bad Debts Written Off	—	−5,000	−1,500
Specific Provision for Doubtful Debts	—	−2,000	—
Debtors for Purposes of Calculating Debt Provision	135,000	183,000	218,500
4% Provision for Doubtful Debts	−5,400	−7,320	−8,740
Debtors for Purpose of Calculating Discount Provision	129,600	175,680	209,760
2% Provision for Discount on Debtors	−2,592	−3,514	−4,195
	127,008	172,166	205,565

Suggested Solution to Question 3.2

(a)   Bad Debts

31.3.95	Debtors	7,500	31.3.95	Profit and Loss	7,500
31.3.96	Debtors	15,000	31.3.96	Profit and Loss	15,000
31.3.97	Debtors	13,000	31.3.97	Profit and Loss	13,000

(b)   Provision for Doubtful Debts

31.3.95	Balance c/d [see Part (e)]	10,100	31.3.95	Profit and Loss	10,100
			1.4.95	Balance b/d	10,100
31.3.96	Balance c/d (£4,000 + £9,800)	13,800	31.3.96	Profit and Loss	3,700
		13,800			13,800
31.3.97	Profit and Loss	3,200	1.4.96	Balance b/d	13,800
	Balance c/d [see Part (e)]	10,600			
		13,800			13,800

(c)   Provision for Discount on Debtors

31.3.95	Balance c/d [see Part (e)]	4,848	31.3.95	Profit and Loss	4,848
31.3.96	Profit and Loss	144	1.4.95	Balance b/d	4,848
	Balance c/d [see Part (e)]	4,704			
		4,848			4,848
			1.4.96	Balance b/d	4,704
31.3.97	Balance c/d [see Part (e)]	5,088	31.3.97	Profit and Loss	384
		5,088			5,088

(d) <u>Profit and Loss Account (extracts) for the Years Ended 31 March (see</u>
   <u>Workings)</u>

	1995	1996	1997
Bad Debts	7,500 Dr.	15,000 Dr.	13,000 Dr.
In/Decrease in Provision for Doubtful Debts	10,100 Dr.	3,700 Dr.	3,200 Cr.
In/Decrease in Provision for Discount on Debtors	4,848 Dr.	144 Cr.	384 Dr.

(e) <u>Balance Sheet (extracts) as at 31 March</u>

	1995	1996	1997
Total Debtors	260,000	264,000	278,000
Bad Debts Written Off	−7,500	−15,000	*−13,000
Specific Provision for Doubtful Debts	—	−4,000	—
Debtors for Purpose of Calculating Debt Provision	252,500	245,000	265,000
4% Provision for Doubtful Debts	−10,100	−9,800	−10,600
Debtors for Purpose of Calculating Disc. Provision	242,400	235,200	254,400
2% Provision for Discount on Debtors	−4,848	−4,704	−5,088
	237,552	230,496	249,312

*£4,000 + £9,000

Workings

<u>Charges to the Profit and Loss Account</u>

	1995	1996	1997
Year-end Provisions for Doubtful Debts (above):			
General Provision	10,100	9,800	10,600
Specific Provision	—	4,000	—
Total	10,100	13,800	10,600
Increase/(Decrease) relative to Previous Year	10,100	3,700	−3,200
Year-end Provision for Discount on Debtors	4,848	4,704	5,088
Increase/(Decrease) relative to Previous Year	4,848	−144	384

Suggested Solution to Question 3.3

(i)   Provision for Bad Debts

Dec 31	P & L – Reduction in Provision	3,455	Jan 1	Balance b/d		4,900
Dec 31	Balance c/d (W1)	6,445	Dec 31	P & L – Increase in Provision		5,000
		9,900				9,900

(ii)   Profit and Loss Account

Dec 31	Bad Debts (4,500 + 5,900)	10,400	Charge
	Reduction in year-end Provision	3,455	Credit
	Increase In Provision during the year	5,000	Charge
	Net	11,945	Charge

W1   Calculation of Provision for Bad Debts as at 31 December 1996

	Amount	Rate	Bad Debt Provision
Debtors 4 Months Old and Older (excl. Bad Debt)	£7,000	30%	£2,100
Debtors Over 3 Months and Less than 4 Months Old	8,000	25%	2,000
All Other Debtors [£12,000 + £21,000 + £13,900]	46,900	5%	2,345
			6,445

(iii)   Extract from Balance Sheet as at 31 December 1996

Debtors (£67,800 – £5,900)	£61,900
Provision for Bad Debts	−6,445
	55,455

(b) The Prudence concept means that revenue and profits are not anticipated. They are included in the Profit and Loss Account only when realised, either in the form of cash, or of other assets, the ultimate cash realisation of which can be assessed with reasonable certainty.

Provision is made for all liabilities, both expenses and losses, as soon as they become known, unless the expenses relate to a future period and it is reasonably certain that they will give rise to future revenue, greater than or equal to, the amount of the expenses. If the amount of an expense to be provided for is not known with certainty, an estimate should be made in the light of available information.

Where the prudence concept and the accruals concept conflict, the prudence concept takes precedence.

Section 4

Accruals and Prepayments

Suggested Solution to Question 4.1

Rent and Rates

Dec 31	Bank – Rent	3,600	Jan 1	Balance b/d (Rates Accrued)		360
	Bank – Rates	2,400	Dec 31	Profit and Loss		*6,420
Dec 31	Balance c/d (Rent Accrued)	1,200	Dec 31	Balance c/d (Rates Prepaid)		420
		7,200				7,200

* Rent payable for 1996 = £1,200 × 4			£4,800
Rates payable for 1996 =			
1 January to 31 March 1996 = £720 × 3/6	£360		
1 April to 30 September 1996	840		
1 October to 31 December 1996 = £840 × 3/6	420	1,620	
Total Charge to Profit and Loss Account			6,420

Suggested Solution to Question 4.2

Rent and Rates

1.10.95	Balance b/d (Rates Prepaid)	7,500	1.10.95	Balance b/d (Rent Accrued)		6,000
3.10.95	Bank – Rent	6,000				
5.1.96	Bank – Rent	6,000				
4.4.96	Bank – Rent	6,000				
27.5.96	Bank – Rates	9,000				
10.7.96	Bank – Rent	6,000				
30.9.96	Balance c/d (Rent Accrued)	10,000	30.9.96	Profit and Loss		*44,500
		50,500				50,500

*Rent:	9 Months × £24,000 per annum		18,000	
	3 Months × £40,000 per annum		10,000	28,000
Rates	6 Months × £15,000 per annum		7,500	
	6 Months × £18,000 per annum		9,000	16,500
Charge to Profit and Loss Account				44,500

Suggested Solution to Question 4.3

Rent and Rates

Jan 1	Balance b/d (Rent Prepaid)	6,000	Jan 1	Balance b/d (Rates Accrued)	6,000
Feb 1	Bank (Rent)	18,000	Dec 31	Profit and Loss	*102,500
Mar 31	Bank (Rates)	12,000			
May 1	Bank (Rent)	18,000			
Aug 1	Bank (Rent)	21,000			
Sep 30	Bank (Rates)	12,000			
Nov 1	Bank (Rent)	21,000			
Dec 31	Balance c/d (Rates Accrued)	7,500	Dec 31	Balance c/d (Rent Prepaid)	7,000
		115,500			115,500

Proof of Profit and Loss Account Charge

Rent: 1 January to 31 July = 7 Months

    × £72,000 per annum   £42,000

    1 August to 31 December = 5 Months

    × £84,000 per annum   35,000

                    77,000

Rates: 1 January to 30 September = 9 Months

    × £24,000 per annum   £18,000

    1 October to 31 December = 3 Months

    × £30,000 per annum   7,500   25,000

                    102,500

Suggested Solution to Question 4.4

Rent and Rates

Jan. 1	Balance b/d (rates prepaid)	2,000	Jan. 1	Balance b/d (rent accrued)		4,000
Feb. 1	Bank – Rent	6,000	Dec. 31	Profit and Loss		*33,000
May 1	Bank – Rates	4,400				
May 2	Bank – Rent	6,000				
Aug. 14	Bank – Rent	6,000				
Oct. 12	Bank – Rates	4,400				
Nov. 11	Bank – Rent	6,000				
Dec. 31	Balance c/d (rent accrued)	4,400	Dec. 31	Balance c/d (rates prepaid)		2,200
		39,200				39,200

*Rent: 10 Months × £2,000 per month   £20,000

     2 Months × £2,200 per month   4,400

                      24,400

Rates: 3 Months to 31 March 1996   £2,000

     9 Months to 31 December 1996

      (£8,000 + £800) × 9/12   6,600   8,600

    Charge to the Profit and Loss Account   33,000

Suggested Solution to Question 4.5

Rent Receivable

Dec 31	Profit and Loss A/c (W1)	8,411	Dec 31	Bank (W1)	8,681
Dec 31	Balance c/d (693 + 336)	1,029	Dec 31	Balance c/d	759
		9,440			9,440

W1 Income for the Year and Balances at the end of the Year

			Income	Received	Balance
Flat 1:					
Jan–Mar	3 Months × £210	630			
Apr–Dec	9 Months × (£210 × 110%)	2,079	2,709	3,402	693
Flat 2:		880			
Jan–Apr	4 Months × £220				
Jul–Dec	6 Months × (£220 × 115%)	1,518	2,398	1,639	−759
Flat 3:		280			
Jan	1 Month × £280				
Mar–Aug	6 Months × £280	1,680			
Sept–Dec	4 Months × (£280 × 120%)	1,344	3,304	3,640	336
Income to be Shown in Profit and Loss Account			8,411	8,682	270

Suggested Solution to Question 4.6

(a)   Provision for Major Overhauls

31.12.93	Balance c/d	840,000	31.12.93	Profit and Loss	840,000
	Bank	1,500,000	1.1.94	Balance b/d	840,000
31.12.94	Balance c/d	270,000	31.12.94	Profit and Loss	930,000
		1,770,000			1,770,000
			1.1.95	Balance b/d	270,000
31.12.95	Balance c/d	1,140,000	31.12.95	Profit and Loss	870,000
		1,140,000			1,140,000
	Bank	1,500,000	1.1.96	Balance b/d	1,140,000
31.12.96	Balance c/d	600,000	31.12.96	Profit and Loss	960,000
		2,100,000			2,100,000

Cost of Major Overhaul	£1,500,000
No. of Hours Per Overhaul	10,000

Therefore, Charge Per Flying Hour (£1,500,000/10,000 hours)   £150

Calculation of Charge to the Profit and Loss Account

Year	No. of Hours Flown	Charge per Hour	Total Charge
1993	5,600	£150	£840,000
1994	6,200	150	930,000
1995	5,800	150	870,000
1996	6,400	150	960,000

(b) The balance on the account (if any) will represent an accrued expense and, as such, should be shown as a current liability in the Balance Sheet.

Section 5

The Valuation of Stock

Suggested Solution to Question 5.1

The First In, First Out (FIFO) Method of Approximating the Cost of Stock ensures that materials are issued at actual cost. Therefore, no profits or losses will be shown as a result of adopting this price. Under this method, it is assumed that materials purchased are issued (for the purposes of valuing them) in strict chronological order. FIFO is easy to operate but, if the price of materials purchased fluctuates considerably, it involves a number of tedious calculations, which may increase the possibility of errors. A great advantage of FIFO is that not only is stock shown at actual cost but it is as closely representative of current prices as possible. When prices are falling the material charge to production is high, while the replacement cost of stock will be low. Conversely, when prices are rising, the charge to production will be low, while the replacement cost will be high.

Suggested Solution to Question 5.2

The Last In, First Out (LIFO) Method of Approximating the Cost of Stock also ensures that materials are issued at actual cost. It is assumed that the materials purchased are issued in the reverse order of FIFO, i.e. the last receipt is the first issue. Again, if the price of the materials purchased fluctuates considerably, it involves a number of tedious calculations. Although stock is shown at cost, the price is that of the oldest material in store, so it may not represent current price levels. Consequently, it may be necessary to write off stock losses during periods of falling prices as the book values of materials will exceed the market values. A great advantage of this method is that the charge to production is as closely related to current price levels as possible. Assuming the purchase of materials was in recent times, it will not be necessary to ascertain market values.

Suggested Solution to Question 5.3

Use of the Average Cost Method of Approximating the Cost of Stock to value material issues means that an approximate figure is obtained, owing to the fact that the total of the prices paid for the materials is divided by the number of prices used in the calculation. Materials are therefore not charged out at actual cost, so a profit or loss may be shown merely by adopting this price when valuing materials charged to production. There are different methods of calculating average cost, each of them varying in complexity. The one just described is the Simple Average Cost method. The Weighted Average Cost method is similar except that total quantities and total cost are considered. Under this method issue prices are calculated upon receipt of materials, not upon issue. Finally, the periodic Simple Average Price is derived, by dividing the total price of the materials obtained during that period, by the number of prices used in the calculation.

Suggested Solution to Question 5.4

Statement of Standard Accounting Practice No. 9 requires that stock should be included in the accounts at the lower of its cost and its net realisable value. This means that if stock on hand could only be resold at a price lower than its initial cost, then it should be valued in the accounts by reference to this lower amount. The reason for this lies in the fundamental accounting concept of prudence in that all foreseeable losses should be provided for in the accounts as soon as possible, and that gains are recognised in the accounts only when realised in the form of cash or cash equivalents, whose value can be ascertained with reasonable certainty.

Suggested Solution to Question 5.5

Raw Material Stocks should be valued on the FIFO basis, i.e. the calculation of the cost of raw materials on the basis that the quantities in hand represent the latest purchases of production. This is as required by SSAP 9 'Stocks and Long-term Contracts'.

The LIFO basis, in general, can result in the reporting of current assets at amounts that bear little relationship to recent costs and thus provide a misleading and potentially distorting effect on current assets and future results. Since SSAP 9 mandates the use of a method which provides a fair approximation to the expenditure actually incurred, FIFO is more appropriate.

Valuing raw materials at the lower of FIFO or LIFO, is not appropriate, as LIFO, in general, is not regarded as a 'best approximation' valuation method.

Overall, the valuation of raw materials is one that requires professional management judgement, but FIFO appears most appropriate.

Suggested Solution to Question 5.6

In general, stocks of finished goods should be valued at the lower of cost and 'net realisable value' (NRV).

The calculation of cost must take into account all expenditure incurred in the normal course of business in bringing products to their present location and condition. This involves the allocation of overheads, which may be quite arbitrary. A number of options include Job Costing, Batch Costing, Standard Costing etc. SSAP 9 requires the selection of the most appropriate method. NRV means the estimated proceeds from the ultimate sale of the finished goods, less all further costs/expenses before sale.

The prudence concept mentioned in SSAP 2 dictates that stock should not be valued above NRV. Therefore, the valuation of finished goods stocks at the higher of cost and NRV is not appropriate.

Overall, there is a need for consistency in valuation, with an overriding consideration in valuing stock for the accounts to provide a 'True and Fair' view.

Suggested Solution to Question 5.7

(a)   Value of Monthly Closing Stock Using the FIFO Method

Date	Stock Received			Stock Issued			Stock at End of Month		
	Units	Price	Value	Units	Price	Value	Units	Price	Value
25 July	150	£20	£3,000				150	£20	£3,000
28 August	225	£30	£6,750				150	£20	£3,000
							225	£30	6,750
							375		9,750
15 September				150	£20	£3,000			
				155	£30	4,650			
				305		7,650	70	£30	£2,100
4 October				50	£30	£1,500	20	£30	£600
10 November	410	£40	16,400				20	£30	£600
							410	£40	16,400
							430		17,000
23 December				20	£30	£ 600			
				80	£40	3,200			
				100		3,800	330	£40	£13,200

(b)　　　　　　　　Trading and Profit and Loss Account
　　　　　　　　　for the period 1 July to 31 December

Sales [(305 @ £45) + (50 @ £45) + (100 @ £75)]		£23,475
Cost of Sales		
Opening Stock	£ Nil	
Purchases [(150 @ £20) + (225 @ £30) + (410 @ £40)]	26,150	
	26,150	
Closing Stock (per (a) above)	13,200	12,950
Gross Profit		10,525
Expenses (£1,400 per month × 6 months)		8,400
Net Profit		2,125

Balance Sheet as at 31 December

Current Assets		
Bank (W1)		£10,045
Stock [per (a)]		13,200
Debtors (December sales not yet paid		
= 100 units @ £75 + VAT @ 20%)		9,000
		32,245
Current Liabilities		
Trade Creditors (November purchases		
= 410 @ £40 + 10% VAT)	£18,040	
VAT Payable (W2)	2,080	20,120
		12,125
Financed By:		
Capital at the Start of the Year		10,000
Net Profit for the Year		2,125
		12,125

W1   Bank Balance at 31 December

Summary of Money Received and Paid

	Jul £	*Aug* £	*Sep* £	*Oct* £	*Nov* £	*Dec* £
Inflows						
Debtors	—	—	—	16,470	2,700	—
	—	—	—	16,470	2,700	—
Outflows						
Expenses	1,400	1,400	1,400	1,400	1,400	1,400
Creditors	—	—	3,300	7,425	—	—
Total Outflow	1,400	1,400	4,700	8,825	1,400	1,400
Net Cash Flow	−1,400	−1,400	−4,700	7,645	1,300	−1,400
Opening Balance	10,000	8,600	7,200	2,500	10,145	11,445
Closing Balance	8,600	7,200	2,500	10,145	11,445	10,045

W2   VAT Payable as at 31 December
      VAT on Sales:
          Sales of £23,475 × 20%   £4,695
      Deductible VAT on Purchases:
          Purchases of £26,150 × 10%   −2,615
                                                     2,080

Section 6

Bank Reconciliation Statements

Suggested Solution to Question 6.1

Bank

Jun. 30	Balance 'b/d'*	9,936				
Jun. 21	Difference (£5,844 – £5,784)	60	Jun. 25	Standing Order	825
Jun. 30	Difference (£576 – £144)	432	Jun. 30	Balance c/d	9,603
		10,428			10,428

*Balance given (£891) + Lodgements (£54,513) – Cheque Payments (£45,468)

Bank Reconciliation Statement as at 30 June

Revised Balance Per Cash Book		£9,603
Unpresented Cheques:		
No. 500 062	£26,334	
No. 500 063	9,000	
No. 500 066	1,566	36,900
Balance Per Bank Statement		46,503

Suggested Solution to Question 6.2

Bank

Dec 18	Lodgement Understated	110	Dec 31	Balance 'b/d'		288
Dec 16	Cheque No. 508214		Dec 2	Life Assurance Direct		
	overstated	81		Debit		45
Dec 20	Cheque No. 508215		Dec 5	Motor Lease Direct		
	overstated	9		Debit		287
			Dec 5	Cheque No. 508209		
				understated		2
			Dec 12	Cheque Dishonoured		450
			Dec 16	Interest not recorded		315
			Dec 16	Bank Charges not		
				recorded		204
Dec 31	Balance c/d	1,394	Dec 31	Bank Charges not		
				recorded		3
		1,594				1,594

Gerard Knight
Bank Reconciliation Statement as at 31 December

Adjusted Balance per ledger Bank Account (Overdrawn)			£1,394	Cr.
Unpresented Cheques:	No. 508208	£350		
	508210	285		
	508211	487		
	508212	384		
	508216	33	1,539	
Balance per the Bank Statement			145	Cr.

Note

The difference between the opening balance per the bank account of £1,810 overdrawn, and that per the Bank Statement of £1,500 overdrawn, is as follows:

Balance per the Bank Statement (Overdrawn)			£1,500	Dr.
November cheques presented in December:	No. 508204	£125		
	508205	185	310	
Balance per the ledger Bank Account (Overdrawn)			1,810	Cr.

Section 7

Control Accounts

Suggested Solution to Question 7.1

Control accounts act as an independent check of the subsidiary ledgers by comparing the total of the sales or purchases ledger listings at the end of a month with an independently calculated control total.

Suggested Solution to Question 7.2

Debtors Control

Jan. 1	Balance b/d	170,000		Sales Returns	18,000
	Sales	450,000		Bank	410,000
				Discount Allowed	16,000
				Bad Debts	14,000
				Contra – Sam Smith	2,500
Dec. 31	Balance c/d	7,000	Dec. 31	Balance c/d	166,500
		627,000			627,000

Creditors Control

	Purchases Returns	22,000	Jan. 1	Balance b/d	130,000
	Bank	290,000		Purchases	320,000
	Discount Received	25,000			
	Contra – Sam Smith	2,500			
Dec. 31	Balance c/d	121,500	Dec. 31	Balance c/d	11,000
		461,000			461,000

Suggested Solution to Question 7.3

Debtors Control

Jan. 1	Balance b/d	20,000	Jan. 1	Balance b/d	2,000
	Sales	140,000		Sales Returns	8,000
				Bank	120,000
				Discount Allowed	2,000
				Bad Debts	6,000
Dec. 31	Balance c/d	3,000	Dec. 31	Balance c/d	25,000
		163,000			163,000

Creditors Control

Jan. 1	Balance b/d	8,000	Jan. 1	Balance b/d	18,000
	Purchases Returns	4,000		Purchases	90,000
	Bank	75,000			
	Discount Received	3,000			
Dec. 31	Balance c/d	19,200	Dec. 31	Balance c/d	1,200
		109,200			109,200

Suggested Solution to Question 7.4

1.   Calculation of Correct Balance on Debtors Control Account
                        as at 31 March 1997

Original Balance per Control Account		£257,200
Sales Returns Book overcast	(j)	1,000
		258,200
Bad Debt	(d)	−800
Correct Balance		257,400

Calculation of Correct Balance on Creditors Control Account
                        as at 31 March 1997

Original Balance per Control Account		£191,400
Purchases Book Overcast	(a)	−10,000
Goods Returned	(b)	−750
Correct Balance		180,650

2.   Reconciliation of Total per Original List of Debtors' Balances
with Corrected Balance

Total per original list (balancing figure)			£256,100
Add:			
Balance omitted	(f)	£1,300	
Refund to A. Smith	(h)	500	1,800
			257,900
Deduct:			
Credit Balance shown as a debit balance	(c)		500
			257,400

Reconciliation of Total per Original List of Creditors' Balances
with Corrected Balance

Total per original list (balancing figure)			£176,720
Add Purchase from C. Temple	(g)		7,000
			183,720
Deduct:			
Goods Returned	(b)	£750	
Contra J. Kelly	(e)	1,500	
Refund to A. Smith	(h)	500	
Discount Received	(i)	320	−3,070
			180,650

Suggested Solution to Question 7.5

(a)   Computation of Correct Balance per Debtors Control Account
as at 31 December 1996

Original Balance per Control Account			£78,214
Add: Sales Book undercast	(8)		1,000
			79,214
Less:			
Bad Debt	(2)	£600	
Goods Returned	(4)	635	−1,235
			77,979

Computation of Correct Balance per Creditors Control Account
as at 31 December 1996

Original Balance per Control Account			£56,191
Purchases Book Undercast	(10)		900
Discount Received	(7)		−215
			56,876

(b) Reconciliation of Original List of Debtors Balances
with Correct Control Account Balance

Total per Original List (balancing figure)			£74,074
Add:			
Sale to T. Evans	(1)	£4,600	
Refund to P. Moran	(5)	1,200	5,800
			79,874
Less:			
Goods Returned	(4)	635	
Contra C. Smith	(9)	1,260	−1,895
			77,979

Reconciliation of Original List of Creditors Balances
with Correct Control Account Balance

Total per Original List (balancing figure)			£57,801
Add Balance Omitted	(3)		670
			58,471
Less:			
Refund to P. Moran	(5)	£1,200	
Debit Balance Shown as Credit Balance	(6)	180	
Discount Received	(7)	215	−1,595
			56,876

Suggested Solution to Question 7.6

Debtors Control Account for the Period Ended 31 March 1997

Balance b/d	17,370	Blue – Contra (2)	200
		Bank – Net Error (4)	1,310
Sales Returns Overstated (3)	180	Cash Book Understated (7)	680
Bad Debt Recovered		Balance c/d	15,460
Reinstated (9)	100		
	17,650		17,650

List of Balances

Balance Per Original Listing				£16,580
Add	White – Balance Omitted	(Note 5)	£300	
	Bad Debt Recovered Reinstated	(Note 9)	100	400
Less	Black – Balance incorrectly Posted	(Note 1)	500	
	Blue – Contra	(Note 2)	200	
	Yellow – Balance Overstated	(Note 6)	270	
	Bad Debt Written Off	(Note 8)	450	
	Bad Debt Recovered – Amount Received	(Note 9)	100	−1,520
Balance Per Debtors Control Account				15,460

Section 8

Correction of Errors and Suspense Accounts

Suggested Solution to Question 8.1

(a)		Debit	Credit
1.	Sales	£1,700	
	Fixtures and Fittings Disposal A/c		£1,700
	Being proceeds on disposal of fixtures and fittings		
	incorrectly posted to sales A/c		
	Fixtures and Fittings Disposal A/c	£3,400	
	Fixtures and Fittings A/c		£3,400
	Being cost of assets disposed of transferred to disposal		
	A/c		
	Provision for Depreciation A/c	£1,530	
	Fixtures and Fittings Disposal A/c		£1,530
	Being provision for depreciation on assets disposed of		
	transferred to disposal A/c		
	Profit and Loss A/c	£170	
	Fixtures and Fittings Disposal A/c		£170
	Being loss on disposal transferred to Profit and Loss		
	A/c		
2.	Advertising – (Profit and Loss A/c)	£2,800	
	Bank		£2,800
	Being advertising expense recorded in Profit and Loss		
	A/c and bank A/c		
3.	Cash Sales	£4,800	
	Debtors		£4,800
	Being amount received from debtors incorrectly posted		
	to cash sales – transferred to debtors		
4.	Creditors	£3,800	
	Purchases Returns		£3,800
	Being goods purchased returned to suppliers		

(b) Net Profit   £7,800
     Add: Purchases Returns   3,800
                                                                 11,600

     Less
     Sales   £1,700
     Loss on Disposal of Fixtures and Fittings   170
     Advertising   2,800
     Cash Sales   4,800   −9,470
     Revised Net Profit   2,130

Suggested Solution to Question 8.2

Thomas Keynes
(a)   Statement of Corrected Net Loss/Profit

Net Loss per Draft Accounts			£−2,800
Corrections	*Increase in Profit*	*Decrease in Profit*	
1. Reduce Repairs		£2,500	
Increase Depreciation	£250		
2. Decrease Bank Interest and Charges		1,400	
Increase Insurance	600		
3. Increase Motor Expenses	500		
4. Decrease Purchases		1,200	
5. Increase Sales		5,000	
6. Decrease Rent Payable		850	
7. No Effect			
8. Increase Bad Debts	3,800		
Decrease Provision for Doubtful Debts (W1)		700	
Increase Provision for Discount (W2)	1,026		
	6,176	11,650	
Net Effect of Adjustments (Profit)			5,474
Corrected Net Profit			2,674

W1   <u>Decrease in Provision for Doubtful Debts</u>

Debtors	£57,800
Bad Debts	−3,800
	<u>54,000</u>
5%	−2,700
Actual	<u>3,400</u>
Reduce by	<u>700</u>

W2   <u>Increase in Provision for Discount</u>

Debtors net of Bad Debts (W1)	£54,000
Provision for Doubtful Debts	−2,700
	<u>51,300</u>
2%	<u>1,026</u>

(b) Suspense

Jan 31	2. Bank Interest &		Jan 31	2. Insurance	600
	Charges	1,400			
	5. Sales	5,000		7. Sales Ledger	2,500
	5. Capital Introduced	5,000			
	6. Rent Payable	850		Opening Balance	
				(Derived)	9,150
		<u>12,250</u>			<u>12,250</u>

Suggested Solution to Question 8.3

1.   Statement of Corrected Net Profit

Net Profit per Draft Accounts			£13,360
	Profit	*Profit*	
Corrections	*Increase*	*Decrease*	
(a) No Effect			
(b) Reduce Purchases	£7,500		
Increase Depreciation		£750	
(c) Increase Insurance		1,500	
(d) Increase Discount Received	650		
(e) Introduce Bad Debts		2,600	
Reduce Provision for Doubtful			
Debts (W1)	300		
Introduce Provision for Discount			
on Debtors (W2)		646	
(f) No Effect			
(g) No Effect			
(h) Increase Bank Interest		1,300	
Reduce Rent	800		
	9,250	6,796	
Net Increase			2,454
Corrected Net Profit			15,814

W1 Reduce Provision for Doubtful Debts		
Debtors	£36,600	
Bad Debts	−2,600	
	34,000	
5% Provision	−1,700	
Existing Provision	2,000	
Reduction	300	
W2 Introduce Provision for Discount on Debtors		
Debtors Net of Bad Debts (W1)	£34,000	
Provision for Bad Debts	−1,700	
	32,300	
2% Provision	646	

2. Suspense

(a) Capital Introduced	12,000	(c) Insurance	1,500
		(f) Purchases Ledger A/c	1,000
		(g) Sales Ledger A/c	2,250
Drawings	12,000	Opening balance (derived)	19,250
	24,000		24,000

Section 9

Final Accounts of Sole Traders

Suggested Solution to Question 9.1

J. Charleton

(a) Trading and Profit and Loss Account for the Year Ended 31 March 1997

Sales		£750,000
Cost of Sales		
Stock on hand on 1 April 1996	£74,000	
Purchases	465,000	
	539,000	
Stock on hand on 31 March 1997	68,000	471,000
Gross Profit		279,000
Rent Receivable (£12,000 – £9,000 Prepayment)		3,000
		282,000
Expenses		
Wages and Salaries	£87,000	
Motor Expenses	26,500	
Telephone and Postage	8,600	
Light and Heat	17,410	
Rates	6,900	
Insurance (£13,400 – £2,200 Prepayment)	11,200	
Bank Interest and Charges (£18,950 + £5,600 Accrual)	4,550	
Legal Fees (£15,000 per TB – £12,500 Capital Exp.)	2,500	
Accountancy Charges	3,200	
Bad Debts	5,500	
Provision for Doubtful Debts [(£85,000 – £5,500) @ 2%]	1,590	
Miscellaneous Expenses (£8,470 + £4,200 Accrual)	12,670	
Depreciation	13,600	221,220
Net Profit		60,780

J. Charleton

(b) Balance Sheet as at 31 March 1997

Fixed Assets	Cost	Depreciation	NBV
Premises (£220,000 per TB +12,500 legal fees paid +5,000 legal fees accrued)	£237,500	–	£237,500
Vehicles	56,000	22,400	33,600
Equipment	24,000	9,600	14,400
	317,500	32,000	285,500
Current Assets			
Stock		£68,000	
Debtors (£85,000 per TB −£5,500 bad debts)	£79,500		
Provision for Doubtful Debts (2% of above figure)	−1,590	77,910	
Sundry Debtors and Prepayments (£2,200 VAT +£2,200 Insurance)		4,400	
		150,310	
Current Liabilities			
Bank	£16,250		
Creditors	43,500		
Legal Fees Accrual	5,000		
Rent Receivable Prepaid	9,000		
Bank Interest Accrual	5,600		
Miscellaneous Expenses Accrual	4,200	83,550	
Net Current Assets			66,760
			352,260
Long-term Liabilities			
Bank Loan			150,000
			202,260
Financed By:			
Capital at start of year			162,080
Net Profit			60,780
			222,860
Drawings			−20,600
Capital at end of year			202,260

Suggested Solution to Question 9.2

Pat O'Neill

(a) Trading and Profit and Loss Account
for the Year Ended 31 December 1996

Sales		£550,000
Cost of Sales		
Opening Stock	£50,000	
Purchases	300,000	
	350,000	
Closing Stock	65,000	285,000
Gross Profit		265,000
Expenses		
Wages	£80,000	
Rent and Rates	5,000	
Insurance	8,000	
Motor Travel	12,000	
Repairs and Renewals	11,000	
Bank charges (incl. accrual)	3,800	
Bad debts	9,000	
Provision for bad debts	13,500	
Depreciation of Plant and Equipment	9,600	151,900
Net Profit		113,100

Pat O'Neill

(b)   Balance Sheet as at 31 December 1996

Fixed Assets			
Plant and Equipment			£38,400
Current Assets			
Stock		£65,000	
Bank		75,000	
Debtors	£90,000		
Provision for bad and doubtful debts	13,500	76,500	
		216,500	
Current Liabilities			
Creditors	£40,000		
Bank interest and charges accrued	800	−40,800	175,700
			214,100
Financed By			
Capital			116,000
Drawings			−15,000
			101,000
Net Profit for the year			113,100
			214,100

Suggested Solution to Question 9.3

B. Harton

(a)   Trading and Profit and Loss Account
for the Year Ended 31 December 1996

Sales			£746,000
Cost of Sales			
Stock on hand at start of year		£180,000	
Purchases		556,000	
		736,000	
Stock on hand at end of year		160,000	576,000
Gross Profit			170,000
Rental income (£7,400 received			
− £1,200 Prepayment)			6,200
			176,200
Expenses			
Wages		£68,000	
Rent and Rates (£24,000			
− £6,000 Prepayment)		18,000	
Motor Expenses		16,000	
Insurance		7,600	
Telephone and Postage		8,400	
Light and Heat		6,200	
Bank Interest and Charges		12,800	
Accountancy Charges			
(£3,500 + £1,500 Accrual)		5,000	
Bad Debts		6,000	
Provision for Doubtful Debts			
[(114,000 − 6,000) × 2.5% − 1,500]		1,200	
Miscellaneous Expenses			
(£12,400 + £2,300 Accrual)		14,700	
Depreciation of Plant and Equipment			
(40,000 × 10%)	4,000		
Depreciation of Vehicles			
(60,000 × 20%)	12,000		
Depreciation of Office Equipment			
(8,000 × 10%)	800	16,800	180,700
Net Loss for the year			4,500

B. Harton

(b) Balance Sheet as at 31 December 1996

Fixed Assets	*Cost*	*Depreciation*	*NBV*
Plant and Equipment	£40,000	£8,000	£32,000
Vehicles	60,000	24,000	36,000
Office Equipment	8,000	1,600	6,400
	108,000	33,600	74,400
Current Assets			
Stock		160,000	
Debtors (114,000 − 6,000)	108,000		
Provision for Doubtful Debts			
[(114,000 − 6,000) × 2.5%]	−2,700		
		105,300	
Value Added Tax Receivable		4,800	
Rent Payable Prepaid		6,000	
		276,100	
Current Liabilities			
Bank	£34,500		
Creditors	76,000		
PAYE/PRSI Accrual	6,300		
Rent Receivable Prepaid	1,200		
Accountancy Charges Accrual	1,500		
Miscellaneous Expenses Accrual	2,300	121,800	
Net Current Assets			154,300
			228,700
Long-Term Liability			
Bank Loan			100,000
Net Assets			128,700
Financed By:			
Capital at 1 January 1996			165,000
Drawings (£21,800 + £10,000			
Personal Income Tax)			−31,800
Net Loss			−4,500
			128,700

Suggested Solution to Question 9.4

(a)

T. Hardy
Trading and Profit and Loss Account
for the Year Ended 31 December 1996

Sales			£610,000
Cost of Sales			
Stock on hand on 1 January 1996		£37,200	
Purchases		385,000	
		422,200	
Stock on hand on 31 December 1996		28,500	393,700
Gross Profit			216,300
Expenses			
Wages and Salaries	£48,000		
PAYE/PRSI Paid (excl. Personal			
Income Tax)	26,700		
PAYE/PRSI accrued	2,500	77,200	
Telephone and Postage			
(10,700 + £1,500 Accrual)		12,200	
Motor Expenses (18,400			
+ 1,200 VAT Credit disallowed)		19,600	
Rent and Rates (£13,240			
− £2,400 Prepayment)		10,840	
Light and Heat		11,470	
Insurance		14,150	
Bank Interest and Charges			
(£9,100 + £800 Accrual)		9,900	
Accountancy Fees		2,460	
General Expenses		8,190	
Bad Debts		2,400	
Provision for Doubtful Debts			
[(27,400 − 2,400) × 5%]		1,250	
Depreciation		11,200	180,860
Net Profit			35,440

	T. Hardy		
(b)	Balance Sheet as at 31 December 1996		

Fixed Assets	*Cost*	*Depreciation*	*NBV*
Vehicles	£48,000	£19,200	£28,800
Equipment	16,000	6,400	9,600
	64,000	25,600	38,400
Current Assets			
Stock		28,500	
Debtors (27,400 − 2,400)	25,000		
Provision for Doubtful Debts			
(5% of above figure)	−1,250	23,750	
Rent and Rates		2,400	
VAT Receivable (£3,240 − £1,200)		2,040	
		56,690	
Current Liabilities			
Bank Overdraft	13,740		
Creditors	49,280		
Telephone and Postage Accrued	1,500		
Bank Interest and Charges			
Accrued	800		
PAYE/PRSI Accrued	2,500	67,820	
Net Current Liabilities			−11,130
			27,270
Financed By:			
Capital as at 1 January 1996			18,580
Net Profit			35,440
			54,020
Drawings (18,750 + £8,000			
Personal Income Tax)			−26,750
Capital as at 31 December 1996			27,270

Suggested Solution to Question 9.5

Tony Coakley

(a)   Trading and Profit and Loss Account
for the Year Ended 31 March 1997

Sales (£510,000 − £76,300 VAT)		£433,700
Cost of Sales		
Stock on hand on 1 April 1996	£27,200	
Purchases (£310,800 − £53,200 VAT)	257,600	
	284,800	
Stock on hand on 31 March 1997	29,500	255,300
Gross Profit		178,400
Expenses		
Wages and Salaries (37,470 + 16,700 PAYE/PRSI Paid + 1,500 PAYE/PRSI Due)	£55,670	
Motor Expenses	15,470	
Rent and Rates	5,950	
Telephone and Postage	2,190	
Light and Heat	4,010	
Repairs and Renewals	1,750	
Insurance (£2,460 − £660 Prepaid)	1,800	
Bank Interest and Charges (£2,140 + £660 Accrued)	2,800	
Stationary and Advertising (3,430 − 450 VAT)	2,980	
Accountancy Charges (£1,570 + £550 Accrued)	2,120	
Bad Debts	4,400	
Provision for Doubtful Debts [(51,400 − 4,400 Bad) × 2.5%]	1,175	
Depreciation	15,430	115,745
Net Profit		62,655

Tony Coakley
(b) Balance Sheet as at 31 March 1997

Fixed Assets	*Cost*	*Depreciation*	*Net*
Vehicles	£66,000	£26,400	£39,600
Fixtures and Fittings	15,600	3,120	12,480
Office Equipment	6,700	1,340	5,360
	88,300	30,860	57,440
Current Assets			
Stock		29,500	
Trade Debtors (51,400			
− 4,400 Bad)	47,000		
Provision for Doubtful Debts			
(47,000 × 2.5%)	−1,175	45,825	
Prepayments		660	
		75,985	
Current Liabilities			
Trade Creditors	43,200		
PAYE/PRSI Accrued	1,500		
Bank Interest and Charges			
Accrued	660		
Accountancy Charges Accrued	550		
Bank	9,410	55,320	
Net Current Assets			20,665
Net Assets			78,105
Financed By:			
Capital as at 1 April 1996			43,450
Net Profit			62,655
			106,105
Drawings (18,400 + 9,600 Income			
Tax Paid)			−28,000
Capital as at 31 March 1997			78,105

Section 10

Final Accounts of Companies

Suggested Solution to Question 10.1

(a)

Keogh Limited
Trading and Profit and Loss Account
for the Year Ended 31 December 1996

Sales		£286,000
Cost of Sales		
Opening stock	£60,000	
Purchases	160,000	
	220,000	
Closing stock	−85,000	135,000
Gross Profit		151,000
Expenses		
Wages	£30,000	
Rent and rates (£5,000 per TB + £6,000 accrued)	11,000	
Administration expenses	15,000	
Selling and distribution	18,000	
Bank interest and charges	4,000	
Bad debts written off	8,000	
Depreciation of premises (£220,000 @ 2%)	4,400	90,400
Net profit for the year		60,600

Keogh Limited
(b)   Profit and Loss Appropriation Account
for the Year Ended 31 December 1996

Net profit for the year		£60,600
Proposed Preference dividends (£20,000 @ 12%)	£2,400	
Proposed Ordinary dividends (150,000 shares		
@ 10p per share)	15,000	17,400
Profit retained for the year		43,200
Profit and loss account at 1 January 1996		105,000
Profit and loss account at 31 December 1996		148,200

Keogh Limited
(c)   Balance Sheet as at 31 December 1996

Fixed Assets			
Premises at cost			£220,000
Provision for depreciation			
[£44,000 per TB + (£220,000 @ 2%)]			−48,400
Net book value			171,600
Current Assets			
Stock		£85,000	
Debtors and prepayments		80,000	
Bank		25,000	
		190,000	
Current Liabilities			
Creditors and accruals	£101,000		
(£95,000 per TB + £6,000 rates)			
Proposed dividends (£2,400 preference			
+ £15,000 ordinary)	17,400	118,400	
Net Current Assets			71,600
			243,200
Financed by:			
Ordinary share capital (50p shares)			75,000
12% Preference share capital (25p shares)			20,000
Profit and Loss Account			148,200
			243,200

Suggested Solution to Question 10.2

Robin Limited

(a)   Statement of Revised Profit for the Year Ended 31 December 1996

Profit per Trial Balance		£79,000
Less		
Reduction in value of stock (£25,000 − £18,000)	£7,000	
Depreciation on new vehicle (£5,000 × 20%)	1,000	
Additional PAYE provision	6,000	
Debenture Interest (£30,000 × 20%)	6,000	−20,000
		59,000
Add		
Transfer of cost of new vehicle from repairs and		
renewals to fixed assets		5,000
		64,000

Robin Limited

(b)   Profit and Loss Appropriation Account
for the year ended 31 December 1996

Adjusted net profit (as per (a) above)		£64,000
Proposed Ordinary Dividends (62,500 × 5p)	£3,125	
Proposed Preference Dividends (£50,000 × 10%)	5,000	−8,125
		55,875
Transfer to general reserve		15,000
		40,875
Profit and loss account at 1 January 1996		87,000
Profit and loss account at 31 December 1996		127,875

Robin Limited

(c) Balance Sheet as at 30 December 1996

Fixed Assets		Cost	Provision for Depreciation	Net Book Value
Premises		£200,000	£40,000	£160,000
Vehicles	W1	40,000	8,000	32,000
		240,000	48,000	192,000
Current Assets				
Stock (£90,000 − £7,000)			83,000	
Debtors and Prepayments			130,000	
			213,000	
Current Liabilities				
Creditors and Accruals per Trial Balance		80,000		
Additional PAYE Provision		6,000		
Proposed Dividends		8,125		
Debenture Interest Payable (£30,000 × 20%)		6,000		
Bank Overdraft		33,000	133,125	
Net Current Assets				79,875
Net Assets				271,875
Financed By:				
Ordinary share capital (40p shares)				25,000
Preference share capital (50p shares)				50,000
				75,000
General Reserve				39,000
Profit and Loss Account				127,875
				241,875
20% Debentures 2001				30,000
				271,875

Workings

W1 <u>Vehicles</u>

	Cost	Provision for Depreciation	Net Book Value
per Trial Balance	35,000	7,000	28,000
New vehicles	5,000	1,000	4,000
	40,000	8,000	32,000

Suggested Solution to Question 10.3

Timber Ltd.

(a)   Trading and Profit and Loss Account for the Year Ended 31 March 1997

Sales (£5,120,000 – £20,000 Asset disposal proceeds)		£5,100,000
Cost of Sales (£2,880,000 – £80,000 stock error +£120,000 goods not yet delivered)		2,920,000
Gross Profit		2,180,000
Profit on sale of vehicle (£20,000 proceeds – £15,000 NBV)		5,000
		2,185,000
Expenses		
Wages and Salaries	£450,000	
Distribution Costs	120,000	
Administration Costs	180,000	
Rent and Rates (£180,000 + 2/12 × £18,000 for showroom – £25,000 rates prepaid)	158,000	
Light and Heat	30,000	
Insurance	240,000	
Advertising	50,000	
Bad Debts	30,000	
Increase in Provision for Bad Debts {[(£750k – £30k bad) @ 5%] – £30k}	6,000	
Depreciation of Vehicles [(£900,000 – £30,000) × 20%]	174,000	
Depreciation of Plant and Machinery (£1,500,000 × 10%]	150,000	
Depreciation of Buildings (2% of £1,800,000)	36,000	1,624,000
Net Profit for the Year		561,000

Timber Ltd.

Profit and Loss Appropriation Account for the Year Ended 31 March 1997

Net Profit for the Year	£561,000
Dividends (£90,000 Paid + £150,000 Proposed)	–240,000
	321,000
Profit and loss account at 1 April 1996	870,000
Profit and loss account at 31 March 1997	1,191,000

Timber Ltd.
(b)   Balance Sheet as at 31 March 1997

Fixed Assets			
Buildings (£1,350,000 – £36,000 depreciation for the current year)			£1,314,000
Plant and Machinery (£780,000 – £150,000 depreciation for the current year)			630,000
Vehicles [£360,000 – £15,000 = £345,000 – 20% of (£900,000 – £30,000)]			171,000
			2,115,000
Current Assets			
Stock (£780,000 + £80,000 error in stock sheets)		£860,000	
Debtors (£750,000 gross – £30,000 bad – £36,000 provision)		684,000	
Prepayments (Rates)		25,000	
		1,569,000	
Current Liabilities			
Bank	£90,000		
Creditors	750,000		
Accruals (2 months' rent @ £18,000 p.a.)	3,000		
Dividends Payable	150,000	993,000	
Net Current Assets			576,000
Net Assets			2,691,000
Financed By:			
Ordinary Share Capital			1,500,000
Profit and Loss Account			1,191,000
			2,691,000

Suggested Solution to Question 10.4

Caruth Ltd.

(a)   Trading and Profit and Loss Account
for the Year Ended 31 December 1996

Sales		£890,000
Cost of Sales		
Opening Stock	£60,000	
Purchases (£620,000 – Van error £20,000		
– Capital expenditure £1,500)	598,500	
Closing Stock	80,000	578,500
Gross Profit		311,500
Bad debt recovered		4,000
		315,500
Expenses		
Wages and Salaries	£95,000	
Rent (Annual charge = £8,000 or £12,000		
– £4,000 prepaid)	8,000	
Advertising	40,000	
Printing and Stationery	14,000	
Professional Fees	28,000	
Directors' Fees	30,000	
Telephone/Fax expenses	22,000	
Debenture interest (10% of £60,000)	6,000	
Depreciation of Vehicles		
[(£65,000 + £20,000 + £1,500) × 20%]	17,300	
Depreciation of Plant and Machinery		
(£95,000 × 10%]	9,500	
Depreciation of Buildings (2% of £200,000)	4,000	273,800
Net Profit		41,700

Caruth Ltd.

Profit and Loss Appropriation Account for the Year Ended 31 December 1996

Net Profit		£41,700
Dividends		
Ordinary final	£10,000	
Preference interim	5,000	
Preference final	5,000	20,000
		21,700
Profit and loss account at 1 January 1996		178,000
Profit and loss account at 31 December 1996		199,700

	Caruth Ltd.
(b)	Balance Sheet as at 31 December 1996

Fixed Assets

Buildings (£180,000 − £4,000 depreciation for the current year)			£176,000
Land			200,000
Plant and Machinery (£95,000 − £9,500 depreciation for the current year)			85,500
Vehicles (£65,000 − £17,300 depreciation for the current year + £21,500 addition)			69,200
			530,700

Current Assets

Stock		£80,000	
Debtors (£120,000 + £4,000 bad debt recovered − £8,000 provision)		116,000	
Bank		15,000	
Rent Prepaid (6 months × £8,000 p.a.)		4,000	
		215,000	

Current Liabilities

Debenture interest payable	6,000		
Creditors	135,000		
Directors' Fees accrued	30,000		
Dividends Payable (final pref. £5,000 + final ordinary £10,000)	15,000	186,000	29,000
Net Assets			559,700

Financed By:

Ordinary Share Capital	200,000
Preference Share Capital	100,000
10% Debentures 2001	60,000
Profit and Loss Account	199,700
	559,700

Suggested Solution to Question 10.5

Hall Ltd.

(a) Trading and Profit and Loss Account for the Year Ended 31 May 1997

Sales		£610,000
Cost of Sales		420,000
Gross Profit		190,000
Profit on sale of machine (£2,800 proceeds – £1,700 NBV)		1,100
		191,100
Expenses		
Debenture interest (£50,000 × 10%)	£5,000	
Wages and Salaries	84,000	
Rent, Rates and Insurance (£1,200 per TB		
– 6 months rates prepaid @ £600 p.a.)	900	
Directors Remuneration	4,000	
Administrative Costs (£7,100 – £1,000 paid to		
director)	6,100	
Light and Heat	2,400	
Audit Fees (£1,500 + £2,000 accrual)	3,500	
Bad debts	1,800	
Increase in provision for bad debts		
{[(£53,000 – £1,800 bad) @ 5%] – £2,000}	560	
Depreciation of Machinery [(£200,000 – £4,000)		
@ 20%]	39,200	
Depreciation of Vehicles (£15,000 @ 20%)	3,000	150,460
Net Profit		40,640
Dividends		
Interim Ordinary	2,000	
Final Ordinary (400,000 shares @ 3p)	12,000	
Interim Preference	1,000	
Final Preference [(£20,000 @ 10%) – £1,000 interim		
dividend paid)	1,000	16,000
		24,640
Profit and loss account at 1 June 1996		9,400
Profit and loss account at 31 May 1997		34,040

Hall Ltd.

(b)   Balance Sheet as at 31 May 1997

Fixed Assets

Machinery [£127,000 NBV – £1,700 NBV of disposal – 20% of
  (£200,000 cost – £4,000 disposal)]   £86,100

Vehicles [£15,000 – £3,000 depreciation (20% of book value)]   12,000

                                                     98,100

Current Assets

Stock		£220,000
Trade Debtors (£53,000 – £1,800 bad		
= £51,200 – £2,560 provision)		48,640
Other Debtors (machine)		2,800
Loan to director		1,000
Prepayments (6 months rates × £600 p.a.)		300
		272,740
Current Liabilities		
Bank Overdraft	£6,400	
Creditors	42,000	
Accruals (audit fees unpaid)	2,000	
Debenture Interest Payable		
(£5,000 – £1,600)	3,400	
Dividends Payable (£12,000		
ordinary + £1,000 preference)	13,000	66,800
Net Current Assets		205,940
Net Assets		304,040

Financed By:

Ordinary Share Capital	200,000
Preference Share Capital	20,000
10% Debentures 2002	50,000
Profit and Loss Account	34,040
	304,040

Suggested Solution to Question 10.6

Candles Ltd.

(a)   Trading Profit and Loss Account for the Year Ended 31 May 1997

Sales			£1,700,000
Cost of Sales (£960,000 per TB + £30,000 stock sheet error			
+ £40,000 goods not delivered)			1,030,000
			670,000
Expenses			
Rent and Rates[1]		£51,000	
Insurance		80,000	
Wages and Salaries		150,000	
Distribution		40,000	
Administration		60,000	
Heat and Light		10,000	
Printing, Postage and Stationery		16,000	
Bad Debts		10,000	
Increase in Provision for Bad Debts			
{[(£250,000 − £10,000 bad) @ 5%]			
− £10,000}		2,000	
Loss on sale of vehicle (£1,000 received			
− £4,000 NBV)		3,000	
Depreciation			
− Vehicles [20% of			
(£299,000 − £20,000)]	£55,800		
− Plant and Machinery			
(10% of £500,000)	50,000		
− Land and Buildings			
(2% of £600,000)	12,000	117,800	539,800
			130,200
Dividends			
Interim Ordinary dividend		25,000	
Final Ordinary dividend		50,000	75,000
Profit retained for the year			55,200
Profit and loss account at 1 June 1996			290,000
Profit and loss account at 31 May 1997			345,200

[1] £60,000 per TB − 2 months rent prepaid @ £6,000 p.a. = £1,000 − 4 months rates prepaid @ £24,000 p.a. = £8,000

Candles Ltd.
(b)   Balance Sheet as at 31 May 1997

Fixed Assets

Land and Buildings (£450,000 − £12,000 current year
  depreciation)   £438,000
Plant and Machinery (£260,000 − £50,000 current year
  depreciation)   210,000
Vehicles[2]   60,200
                                                                    708,200

Current Assets

Stock (£260,000 per TB − £30,000 stock sheet
  error)   £230,000
Debtors (£250,000 per TB − £10,000 bad debts
  − £12,000 provision)   228,000
Prepayments (£1,000 rent prepaid
  + £8,000 rates prepaid per note 1 to P&L
  Account)   9,000
                                               467,000

Current Liabilities

Creditors (£210,000 per TB
  + £40,000 goods not yet
  delivered)   £250,000
Bank Overdraft   30,000
Dividends Payable   50,000   330,000

  Net Current Assets   137,000
  Net Assets   845,200

Financed by:

Ordinary Share Capital   500,000
Profit and Loss Account   345,200
                                                                   845,200

[2] £119,000 − £19,000 (to be credited in respect of £20,000 disposal at cost) + £16,000 depreciation on disposal − £55,800 depreciation for the year ended 31 May 1997

Suggested Solution to Question 10.7

Brackets Ltd.

(a) Trading and Profit and Loss Account for the Year Ended 30 June 1997

Sales (£2,570,000 − £65,000 goods on sale or return − £5,000 error re. vehicle)			£2,500,000
Cost of Sales (£1,440,000 − £50,000 goods on sale or return)			1,390,000
Gross Profit			1,110,000
Expenses			
Rent and Rates (£90,000 − £1,000 rent prepaid − £12,000 rates prepaid)		£77,000	
Insurance		120,000	
Advertising		65,000	
Light and Heat		15,000	
Printing, Postage and Stationery		20,000	
Increase in Prov for Bad Debts {[(£380k − £65k returns − £15k bad) @ 5%] − £12k}		3,000	
Bad Debts		15,000	
Loss on Sale of Vehicle (£8,000 received − £5,000 NBV)		3,000	
Sales Commission [10% of (£2,500,000 − £2,000,000)]		50,000	
Debenture Interest (£100,000 × 10%)		10,000	
Depreciation of Vehicles [20% of (£500,000 − £20,000)]	£96,000		
Depreciation of Land and Buildings (2% of £900,000)	18,000		
Depreciation of Plant and Machinery (10% of £800,000)	80,000	194,000	
Wages and Salaries		320,000	892,000
Net Profit for the year			218,000
Dividends			
Interim Ordinary		40,000	
Final Ordinary		75,000	115,000
			103,000
Profit and loss account at 1 July 1996			338,000
Profit and loss account at 30 June 1997			441,000

Brackets Ltd.
(b)   Balance Sheet as at 30 June 1997

Fixed Assets			
Land and Buildings			£682,000
Plant and Machinery			320,000
Vehicles [£180,000 − £8,000 = £172,000 − depreciation @ 20% of (£500,000 − £20,000)]			76,000
			1,078,000
Current Assets			
Stock (£400,000 + £50,000 goods on sale or return)		£450,000	
Debtors (£380,000 − £65,000 goods on sale or return − £15,000 bad − 5% provision)		285,000	
Prepayments (Rent £1,000 + Rates £12,000)		13,000	
		748,000	
Current Liabilities			
Bank	£55,000		
Creditors	340,000		
Accruals [Commission: 10% of (£2.5m − £2m)]	50,000		
Debenture Interest Payable (£10,000 current + £5,000 b/f)	15,000		
Dividends Payable	75,000	535,000	
Net Current Assets			213,000
			1,291,000
10% Debentures 2003			100,000
Net Assets			1,191,000
Financed By:			
Ordinary Share Capital (Shares of £1 each)			750,000
Profit and Loss Account			441,000
			1,191,000

Section 11

Manufacturing Accounts

Suggested Solution to Question 11.1

Manufacturers Ltd.
Manufacturing Account for the Year Ended 31 December 1996

Cost of Raw Materials Consumed		
Stock of Raw Materials on hand on 1 January 1996		£8,000
Purchases of Raw Materials during 1996		45,000
Carriage in Charged on 1996 Purchases of Raw Materials		2,000
Import Duty Charged on 1996 Purchases of Raw Materials		4,500
Stock of Raw Materials on hand on 31 December 1996		−9,000
		50,500
Direct Labour (26,000 + 3,000 Accrual Required for December (Per Note 2))		29,000
Direct Expenses (3,000 Hire of Special Equipment + 5,000 Royalties)		8,000
Prime Cost		87,500
Factory Overheads		
Loose Tools (£1,000 + £2,000 − £750)	£2,250	
Variable Overheads (Per Question)	11,000	
Fixed Overheads (Per Question)	8,000	
Rent and Rates [(£16,000 − £2,000 Prepaid) * 50%]	7,000	
Light and Heat (£4,000 * 50%)	2,000	
Depreciation of Plant and Machinery (Per Note 1 = 10% of £30,000)	3,000	
Quality Assurance Supervisor's Wages (Per Question)	12,000	45,250
		132,750
Work in Progress at 1 January 1996		6,000
Work in Progress 31 December 1996		−8,000
Production Cost of Goods Completed		130,750

Suggested Solution to Question 11.2

Mr. Murphy
(a)   Manufacturing Account for the Year Ended 31 December 1996

Cost of Raw Materials Consumed		
Opening stock of raw materials		£6,000
Purchases of raw materials		60,000
Closing stock of raw materials		−8,000
Carriage inwards		1,000
		59,000
Direct Labour		55,000
Prime Cost		114,000
Factory Overheads		
Manufacturing Overheads	£16,000	
Depreciation of Machinery	10,000	
Rent [(£12,000 + £500 Accrual) @ 50%]	6,250	32,250
		146,250
Opening Work in Progress		7,000
Closing Work in Progress		−5,000
Production Cost of Goods Completed		148,250

Mr. Murphy
Profit and Loss Account for the Year Ended 31 December 1996

Sales		£150,000
Cost of Sales		
Opening stock of finished goods	£3,300	
Production Cost of Goods Completed		
(per Mfg. A/c)	148,250	
Closing stock of finished goods	−4,400	−147,150
Gross Profit		2,850
Expenses		
Selling and Distribution Overheads	£11,000	
Rent [(£12,000 + £500 Accrual) @ 50%]	6,250	
Increase in Provision for Bad Debts		
[(22,000 × 10%) − 600]	1,600	
Bad Debts	400	
Administration Overheads	10,000	−29,250
Net Loss		−26,400

Mr. Murphy

(b)　　　　　Balance Sheet as at 31 December 1996

Fixed Asset	Cost	Depreciation	Net
Machinery	£40,000	£20,000	£20,000

Current Assets

Stock (8,000 RM + 5,000 WIP			
+ 4,400 FG)		£17,400	
Debtors (22,000 − 10% provision)		19,800	
		37,200	

Current Liabilities

Bank Overdraft	£39,600		
Rent Accrued	500		
Creditors	17,000	−57,100	
Net Current Liabilities			−19,900
Net Assets			100

Financed By:

Capital at the start of the year	28,000
Net Loss for the year	−26,400
Drawings	−1,500
	100

Suggested Solution to Question 11.3

Denis O'Connor

(a)　　Manufacturing Account for the Year Ended 31 December 1996

Cost of Raw Materials Used		
Opening stock of raw materials		£37,000
Purchases		135,000
Carriage inwards		3,000
Closing stock of raw materials		−34,000
		141,000
Direct wages		40,000
Prime Cost		181,000
Factory overheads		
Per question	£50,000	
Depreciation of Premises (£95,000 × 2%)	1,900	
Depreciation of Plant and equipment		
(20% × (£50,000 − £18,000))	6,400	
Rent and Rates [(£4,600/£10,000) × £14,000]	6,440	64,740
		245,740
Opening stock of work-in-progress		28,000
Closing stock of work-in-progress		−32,000
Production cost of goods completed		241,740

Denis O'Connor
Trading and Profit and Loss Account for the Year Ended 31 December 1996

Turnover		£375,000
Cost of Sales		
Opening stock of finished goods	£8,000	
Transferred from manufacturing account	241,740	
Closing stock of finished goods	−6,000	−243,740
Gross Profit		131,260
Expenses		
Administrative Overheads[1]	£40,460	
Selling and distribution overheads[2]	47,100	
Bank interest and charges	2,000	
Bad debts	7,000	96,560
Net Profit		34,700

[1] £35,000 + £5,460 Rent and rates allocated [(£3,900/£10,000) × £14,000]
[2] £45,000 + £2,100 Rent and rates allocated [(£1,500/£10,000) × £14,000]

Denis O'Connor
(b)   Balance Sheet as at 31 December 1996

Fixed Assets	*Cost*	*Dep.*	*NBV*
Premises	£95,000	£20,900	£74,100
Plant and Equipment	50,000	24,400	25,600
	145,000	45,300	99,700
Current Assets			
Debtors (£76,000 − £12,000 provision)		£64,000	
Stock (RM £34,000 + WIP £6,000 + FG £32,000)		72,000	
Prepayments		15,000	
Bank		38,000	
		189,000	
Current Liabilities			
Creditors	56,000		
Accruals	29,000	−85,000	
Net Current Assets			104,000
Net Assets			203,700

Financed By:

Capital at 1 January 1996	188,000
Net Profit for the year	34,700
Drawings during the year	−19,000
	203,700

Suggested Solution to Question 11.4

Selkirk Ltd.

(a)   Manufacturing Account for the Year Ended 31 December 1996

Cost of Raw Materials Consumed

Opening stock of raw materials		£20,000
Purchases (+ Carriage in £1,000 − Returns out £2,000)		249,000
Closing stock of raw materials		−15,000
		254,000
Direct Wages		40,000
Direct Expenses (Royalties)		3,000
Prime Cost		297,000
Manufacturing Overheads		
Indirect wages	£23,000	
Heat and light (75% of £10,000)	7,500	
General expenses (50% of £14,000)	7,000	
Insurance (2/3 of £9,000)	6,000	
Depreciation of Production plant and equipment (10% of £120,000)	12,000	
Indirect production materials	2,000	57,500
		354,500
Work in progress at 1 January		7,000
Work in progress at 31 December		−9,000
Production Cost of Goods Completed		352,500

Selkirk Ltd.

Trading and Profit and Loss Account for the Year Ended 31 December 1996

Turnover (Sales £450,000 – Returns £3,000)		£447,000
Cost of Sales		
Opening stock of finished goods	£31,000	
Goods transferred from manufacturing account	352,500	
Closing stock of finished goods (£32,000 cost		
– £2,000 reduction to NRV)	−30,000	−353,500
Gross Profit		93,500
Expenses		
Salesmen's salaries and commission	£9,000	
Heat and Light (25% of £10,000)	2,500	
Postage and telephone	2,000	
Rental of office space (£12,000 per TB		
– £4,000 prepaid)	8,000	
Office salaries	8,000	
General expenses (50% of £14,000)	7,000	
Insurance (1/3 of £9,000)	3,000	
Depreciation of Office equip.		
(20% of £50,000)	10,000	
Depreciation of Delivery vans		
(20% of £24,000)	4,800	14,800
Bad debts	1,200	
Increase in Provision for bad debts[1]	1,340	
Fees	4,000	−60,840
Profit retained for the year		32,660
Profit and loss account at 1 January 1996		56,000
Profit and loss account at 31 December 1996		88,660

[1] {[(£68,000 Gross – £1,200 Bad debts) @ 5%] – £2,000}

Selkirk Ltd.
(b)   Balance Sheet as at 31 December 1996

Fixed Assets	*Cost*	*Depreciation*	*NBV*
Plant and Machinery	£120,000	£48,000	£72,000
Office equipment	50,000	30,000	20,000
Delivery vans	30,000	10,800	19,200
	200,000	88,800	111,200

Current Assets			
Prepaid Rent		£4,000	
Debtors [(£68,000 Gross − £1,200 Bad debts)			
− 5% Provision]		63,460	
Bank		12,000	
Stock [£15,000 RM + £9,000 WIP			
+ £30,000 FG]		54,000	
		133,460	
Current Liabilities			
Creditors	£52,000		
Fees accrued	4,000	−56,000	77,460
			188,660
Financed By:			
Ordinary Share Capital (£1 shares fully paid)			100,000
Profit and Loss Account			88,660
			188,660

Suggested Solution to Question 11.5

Make-it Ltd.

(a) Manufacturing Account for the Year Ended 30 September 1996

Cost of Raw Materials Consumed		
Opening Stock of Raw Materials		£92,565
Purchases of Raw Materials During the Year		1,618,252
Closing Stock of Raw Materials		−63,187
		1,647,630
Direct Labour		795,157
Prime Cost		2,442,787
Factory Overheads		
Repairs to Plant	£11,827	
Production Manager's Salary	23,437	
Factory Power	213,157	
Depreciation of Plant (25% of £384,487)	96,122	
Light and Heat (7/8)	18,270	
Insurance (7/8)	4,676	
Factory General Expenses	11,925	
Rent and Rates (7/8)	24,570	403,984
Factory Cost of Production		2,846,771
Opening Work in Progress	147,300	
Closing Work in Progress	−137,220	10,080
Production Cost of Goods Completed		2,856,851

Make-it Ltd.

(b)   Trading and Profit and Loss Account
for the Year Ended 30 September 1996

Sales			£3,688,042
Cost of Sales			
Opening Stock of Finished Goods		£450,697	
Transfer from Manufacturing Account		2,856,851	
Closing Stock of Finished Goods		−541,365	−2,766,183
Gross Profit			921,859
Establishment Expenses			
Rent and Rates (1/8)	£3,510		
Light and Heat (1/8)	2,610		
Depreciation of Office Furniture			
(20% of £120,750)	24,150		
Insurance (1/8)	668	−30,938	
Administrative and General Expenses			
General Expenses	53,047		
Salaries	69,457		
Audit Fee	7,875	−130,379	
Financial Expenses			
Discount given for Prompt			
Settlement	25,702		
Reduction in Provision for			
Doubtful Debts*	−7,695	−18,007	
Selling and Distribution Expenses			
Sales Director's Salary	26,250		
Advertising	39,960		
Packaging and Delivery Expenses	30,720	−96,930	−276,254
Net Profit			645,605
* Required Provision (5% of £167,400)	£8,370		
Existing Provision	16,065		
Decrease	7,695		

Suggested Solution to Question 11.6

Tony Ltd.
Manufacturing Account for the Year Ended 31 December 1996

Cost of Raw Materials Consumed		
Opening stock of raw materials.		£49,562
Purchases of raw materials		265,040
Closing stock of raw materials		−53,667
		260,935
Direct Labour (£121,732 + £1,569 Accrual)		123,301
Prime Cost		384,236
Manufacturing Overheads		
Factory manager's wages	£28,019	
Power heat and light [(£92,238 + £3,462 Accrual) × 80%]	76,560	
Rates and insurance [(£69,800 − £10,600 prepayment) × 60%]	35,520	
Deprec. of Plant and machinery {[(£387,600 − £201,800) × 20%] × 70%}	26,012	
Depreciation of Premises [(£370,000 × 2%) × 60%]	4,440	170,551
		554,787
Opening Work in Progress		27,930
Closing Work in Progress		−16,420
Production cost of goods completed		566,297

Tony Ltd.
Trading and Profit and Loss Account for the Year Ended 31 December 1996

Turnover		£876,863
Cost of Sales		
Opening stock of finished goods	£61,070	
Opening stock of finished goods bought-in	987	
Goods transferred from manufacturing account	566,297	
Purchase of packing cases	7,430	
Closing stock of finished goods	−43,407	−592,377
Gross Profit		284,486
Discount received		639
		285,125
Expenses		
Administrative wages	£87,932	
Power heat and light [(£92,238 + £3,462 Accrual) × 20%]	19,140	
Rates and insurance [(£69,800 − £10,600 prepayment) × 40%]	23,680	
Directors fees	15,000	
Debenture interest (£500,000 × 7%)	35,000	
Discount allowed	1,462	
Depreciation of Vehicles (£79,700 × 20%)	15,940	
Deprec. of Plant & Machinery {[(£387,600 − £201,800) × 20%] × 30%}	11,148	
Depreciation of Premises [(£370,000 × 2%) × 40%]	2,960	212,262
Profit before tax		72,863
Corporation tax		−8,200
Profit after tax		64,663
Dividends (£4,000 Preference dividend paid + £20,000 Ordinary dividend proposed)		−24,000
		40,663
Profit and loss account at the Start of the Year		10,030
Profit and loss account at the End of the Year		50,693

Tony Ltd.
Balance Sheet as at 31 December 1996

Fixed Assets	Cost	Depreciation	NBV
Premises	£370,000	£28,800	£341,200
Plant and Machinery	387,600	238,960	148,640
Vehicles	79,700	41,140	38,560
	837,300	308,900	528,400
Current Assets			
Stock (RM £53,667 + WIP £16,420 + FG £43,407)		£113,494	
Debtors		62,731	
Rates and insurance prepaid		10,600	
Bank		34,165	
Cash		13,074	
		234,064	
Current Liabilities			
Creditors	£28,540		
Wages and salaries accrued	1,569		
Dividend payable (Ordinary shares)	20,000		
Corporation tax payable	8,200		
Power, light and heat accrued	3,462	−61,771	
Net Current Assets			172,293
			700,693
Financed by:			
Ordinary share capital			100,000
Preference share capital			50,000
Profit and Loss Account			50,693
			200,693
7% Debentures 2001			500,000
			700,693

Suggested Solution to Question 11.7

Manufacturing Company Ltd.
Manufacturing Account for the Year Ended 31 December 1996

Cost of Raw Materials Consumed		
Stock of Raw Materials on hand on 1 January		£17,000
Purchases of Raw Materials during the year		48,000
Carriage in Charged on Purchases of Raw Materials		1,500
Import Duty Charged on Purchases of Raw Materials		4,800
Stock of Raw Materials on hand on 31 December		−10,000
		61,300
Direct Labour [£38,000 per TB + £4,000 Accrual Required for December (per Note 3)]		42,000
Direct Expenses (Hire of Special Equipment £500 + Royalties on Manufacturing Processes £7,000)		7,500
Prime Cost		110,800
Factory Overheads		
Loose Tools (£1,000 + £3,000 − £800)	£3,200	
Variable Factory Overheads	12,500	
Fixed Factory Overheads	19,000	
Rent and Rates [(£10,000 − £2,000) × 3/4]	6,000	
Light and Heat (£14,000 × 3/4)	10,500	
Depreciation of Plant and Machinery	4,000	
Factory Supervisor's Wages	12,000	67,200
		178,000
Work in Progress at 1 January		5,000
Work in Progress at 31 December		−8,000
Production Cost of Goods Completed		175,000

Section 12

Final Accounts of Non-Profit Organisations

Suggested Solution to Question 12.1

Subscriptions

Balance b/d (full members)	600	Balance b/d (full members)	2,100
Income and expenditure	76,400	Balance b/d (associate members)	300
		Income and expenditure	600
Balance c/d	*1,100	Bank	75,100
	78,100		78,100

Subscriptions receivable for 1996

Full Members [(200 − 2 + 12) × £300]	£63,000	
Associate Members [(100 + 10) × £100]	11,000	
	74,000	
Received	75,100	
Therefore, Subscriptions paid in advance	1,100	

Suggested Solution to Question 12.2

Bunker Golf Club
(a) Income and Expenditure Account for the Year Ended 31 December 1996

Income			
Subscriptions	W1		£15,000
Profit on bar	W2		17,000
Profit on dance (£700 − £500)			200
Green fees			3,000
			35,200
Expenditure			
Wages and salaries		£22,700	
Course repairs		3,000	
Rates (£2,600 + £300 − £500)		2,400	
Light and heat (£1,400 + £200 − £100)		1,500	
Sundry expenses		600	
Depreciation of Clubhouse		500	
Depreciation of Fittings and Furniture		1,000	
Depreciation of Equipment		1,600	
Loss on sale of mower [£500 NBV			
− (£3,000 − £2,700 trade-in)]		200	
Loss on competitions (£2,500 − £3,700)		1,200	34,700
Excess of income over expenditure			500

Bunker Golf Club
(b)   Balance Sheet as at 31 December 1996

Fixed Assets			
Clubhouse (£25,000 – 2% depreciation)			£24,500
Fittings and furniture (£10,000 – 10% depreciation)			9,000
Mowers [(£5,500 at start + £3,000 purchased			
– £500 disposal at NBV) – 20% Deprec.]			6,400
			39,900
Current Assets			
Stock		£8,000	
Subscriptions in arrears		700	
Bank		100	
Rates prepaid		500	
		9,300	
Current Liabilities			
Bar creditors	£4,000		
Subscriptions in advance	500		
Light and heat accrued	200	4,700	
Net Current Assets			4,600
			44,500
Accumulated Fund			
Balance at 1 January 1996 (W4)			44,000
Excess of income over expenditure for the year			500
			44,500

W1   Subscriptions

Balance b/d	400	Balance b/d	300
Income and expenditure*	15,000	Bank	14,900
Balance c/d	500	Balance c/d	700
	15,900		15,900

W2   Bar Trading Account

Sales			£51,000
Cost of Sales			
Opening Stock		£7,000	
Purchases	W3	35,000	
Closing Stock		8,000	34,000
Gross Profit			17,000

W3   Bar Creditors Control

Bank	36,000	Balance b/d (creditors)	5,000
Balance c/d	4,000	Credit purchases*	35,000
	40,000		40,000

Bunker Golf Club
W4   Statement of Affairs as at 1 January 1996

Fixed Assets			
Clubhouse (2)			£25,000
Fittings and Furniture (2)			10,000
Mowers (2)			5,500
			40,500
Current Assets			
Bar Stock (1)		£7,000	
Subscriptions in arrears (1)		400	
Rates prepaid (1)		300	
Bank (Receipts and Payments)		1,200	
		8,900	
Liabilities			
Bar Creditors	£5,000		
Subscriptions in advance	300		
Light and heat accrued	100	5,400	3,500
Accumulated Fund at 1 January 1996			44,000

Suggested Solution to Question 12.3

South Yard Football Club

(a)　　　Bar Trading and Profit and Loss Account
for the Year Ended 31 December 1996

Sales		£56,000
Cost of Sales		
Stock on hand on 1 January 1996	£7,500	
Purchases (W1)	39,900	
	47,400	
Stock on hand on 31 December 1996	5,600	41,800
Gross Profit		14,200
Expenses		
Bar Wages	£2,200	
Light and Heat (£2,400 × 50%)	1,200	
Telephone (£650 × 50%)	325	
Insurance (£6,600 (W2) × 50%)	3,300	
Miscellaneous Expenses (£5,400 × 50%)	2,700	
Depreciation (£850 × 50%)	425	10,150
Net Profit		4,050

South Yard Football Club

(b) Income and Expenditure Account for the Year Ended 31 December 1996

Income		
Members' Subscriptions (W3)		£7,300
Bar Profit		4,050
		11,350
Expenditure		
Light and Heat (£2,400 × 50%)	£1,200	
Telephone (£650 × 50%)	325	
Insurance (£6,600 (W2) × 50%)	3,300	
Miscellaneous Expenses (£5,400 × 50%)	2,700	
Net Tour Cost (W4)	2,000	
Depreciation (£850 × 50%)	425	9,950
Surplus of Income over Expenditure		1,400

South Yard Football Club
Balance Sheet as at 31 December 1996

Fixed Assets			
Buildings (£30,000 NBV at 1 Jan. + £7,500 Additions)			£37,500
Furniture and Equipment (£8,500 NBV at 1 Jan.			
− £850 Depreciation)			7,650
			45,150
Current Assets			
Bar Stock		£5,600	
Insurance Prepaid		1,200	
		6,800	
Current Liabilities			
Bank	£3,900		
Bar creditors	2,900		
Subscriptions in Advance	850	7,650	
Net Current Liabilities			850
			44,300
Financed By:			
Accumulated Fund as at			
1 January 1996	W5		42,900
Surplus of Income over			
Expenditure			1,400
Accumulated Fund as at			
31 December 1996			44,300

Workings

W1   Bar Purchases

	Bank	40,100	1 Jan	Balance b/d		3,100
31 Dec	Balance c/d	2,900		Trading Account		
				(derived)		39,900
		43,000				43,000

W2   Insurance

1 Jan	Balance b/d	1,400		P & L/I & E	
				(derived)	6,600
	Bank	6,400	31 Dec	Balance c/d	1,200
		7,800			7,800

W3			Subscriptions	
Income and Exp. (derived)	7,300	1 Jan	Balance b/d	750
31 Dec Balance c/d	850		Bank	7,400
	8,150			8,150

W4   Net Tour Cost

Total Cost		£17,500
Members' Contributions	£7,100	
Fund-raising	8,400	15,500
		2,000

W5   Accumulated Fund as at 1 January 1996

Assets

Premises		£30,000
Furniture and Equipment		8,500
Bar Stock		7,500
Insurance Prepaid		1,400
		47,400

Liabilities

Bank Overdraft	£650	
Bar Creditors	3,100	
Subscriptions in Advance	750	4,500
		42,900

Suggested Solution to Question 12.4

Crookstown Golf Club

(a) Statement of Affairs as at 31 December 1995

Fixed Assets			
Clubhouse			£18,000
Equipment			10,400
			28,400
Current Assets			
Restaurant Stock		£850	
Rates Prepaid		200	
Cash		75	
		1,125	
Current Liabilities			
Bank Overdraft	£1,200		
Light and Heat Accrued	250		
Restaurant Creditors	1,600	3,050	
Net Current Liabilities			1,925
Life Subscriptions Fund			900
			25,575
Financed By:			
Accumulated Fund (balancing figure)			25,575

Crookstown Golf Club

(b) Restaurant Trading and Profit and Loss Account
for the Year Ended 31 December 1996

Sales			£13,800
Cost of Sales			
Opening Stock		£850	
+ Purchases	W1	8,400	
− Closing Stock		−930	−8,320
Gross Profit			5,480
Expenses			
Restaurant Expenses		£750	
Light and Heat	W2	930	
Rent and Rates	W2	740	
Wages and Salaries of Restaurant Staff		3,800	6,220
Net Loss			740

Crookstown Golf Club
(c) Income and Expenditure Account for the Year Ended 31 December 1996

Income			
Subscriptions for 1996 – Ordinary Members (W3)			£11,400
Subscriptions for 1996 – Associate Members (W4)			1,600
Life Subscriptions (W5)			180
Donations Received			950
Deposit Interest (£1,220 – £1,200)			20
			14,150
Expenditure			
Staff Wages		£8,300	
Rent and Rates	W2	740	
Light and Heat	W2	930	
Bank Interest		240	
Depreciation	W6	2,400	
Loss on Restaurant		740	13,350
Surplus of Income over Expenditure			800

Crookstown Golf Club
(d) Balance Sheet as at 31 December 1996

Fixed Assets			
Clubhouse			£18,000
Equipment	W6		9,600
			27,600
Current Assets			
Bank Current Account		£315	
Cash		40	
Subscriptions receivable		400	
Rates Prepaid		320	
Restaurant Stock		930	
		2,005	
Current Liabilities			
Light and Heat Accrued	£310		
Restaurant Creditors	1,400	1,710	
Net Current Assets			295
Net Assets			27,895
Accumulated Fund			
Balance at 31 December 1995			25,575
Surplus of Income over Expenditure			800
			26,375
Life Subscriptions Fund	W5		1,520
			27,895

Workings

W1 Creditors Control

	Cash/Bank	8,600	Jan 1	Balance b/d		1,600
Dec 31	Balance c/d	1,400		Purchases		8,400
		10,000				10,000

W2 Rent and Rates

Jan 1	Balance b/d	200	Dec 31	Restaurant Trading A/c*	740
			Dec 31	Income and Expenditure*	740
Dec 31	Cash/Bank	1,600	Dec 31	Balance c/d	320
		1,800			1,800

Light and Heat

Dec 31	Cash/Bank	1,800	Jan 1	Balance b/d	250
			Dec 31	Restaurant Trading A/c*	930
Dec 31	Balance c/d	310	Dec 31	Income and Expenditure*	930
		2,110			2,110

* 50% charged to the Restaurant and 50% to the rest of the club

W3 Subscriptions – Ordinary Members

Jan 1	Balance b/d	Nil	Dec 31	Cash/Bank	11,000
Dec 31	Income and Expenditure	11,400	Dec 31	Balance c/d	400
		11,400			11,400

W4 Subscriptions – Associate Members

Jan 1	Balance b/d	Nil	Dec 31	Cash/Bank	1,600
Dec 31	Income and Expenditure	1,600	Dec 31	Balance c/d	Nil
		1,600			1,600

W5   Subscriptions – Life Members

Dec 31	Income and Expenditure 10% of (£1,000 + £800)	180	Jan 1	Balance b/d	900
Dec 31	Balance c/d	1,520	Dec 31	Cash/Bank	800
		1,700			1,700

W6   Depreciation

NBV of Equipment at 31 December 1995	£10,400
New Computer	1,600
	12,000
Depreciation @ 20%	2,400
NBV at 31 December 1996	9,600

Suggested Solution to Question 12.5

Greenogue Rugby Club
(a)   Statement of Affairs as at 30 June 1996

Fixed Assets			
Clubhouse			£15,000
Equipment			9,300
			24,300
Current Assets			
Rates prepaid		£300	
Insurance prepaid		400	
Bar stock		2,300	
Bank		1,100	
Cash		150	
		4,250	
Current Liabilities			
Electricity accrued	£250		
Bar creditors	1,800	−2,050	
Net Current Assets			2,200
Net Assets			26,500
Financed By:			
Accumulated Fund			26,500

Greenogue Rugby Club

(b)   Bar Trading Account for the Year Ended 30 June 1997

Sales		£14,200
Cost of Sales		
Opening Bar Stock	£2,300	
+ Purchases (£1,900 Closing − £1,800 opening		
+ £8,400 paid)	8,500	
− Closing Bar Stock	−2,600	−8,200
Gross Profit		6,000
Bar Expenses	620	
Wages and Salaries	4,200	4,820
Net Profit		1,180

Greenogue Rugby Club

(c)   Income and Expenditure Account for the Year Ended 30 June 1997

Income		
Ordinary Subscriptions for 1996/97 [£9,800 ('97) + £800 ('98)		
− £800]		£9,800
Associate Subscriptions for 1996/97		1,200
Life Subscriptions (£600/10 years)		60
		11,060
Profit on Dinner Dance (Tickets £1,500 + Raffle £230		
− Expenses £400)		1,330
Profit on Bar		1,180
		13,570
Expenditure		
Light and Heat (£1,400 + £320 − £250)	£1,470	
Rent and Rates (£2,000 + £300 − £350)	1,950	
Insurance (£780 + £400 − £350)	830	
Wages and Salaries (excl. Bar)	8,090	
Repairs to Clubhouse	630	
Bank interest and Charges	320	
Depreciation W1	1,480	14,770
Excess of Expenditure over Income		1,200

Greenogue Rugby Club
(d)   Balance Sheet as at 30 June 1997

Fixed Assets			
Clubhouse			£15,000
Equipment (W1)			9,720
Computer (W1)			1,600
			26,320
Current Assets			
Cash		£60	
Rates prepaid		350	
Insurance prepaid		350	
Bar Stock		2,600	
		3,360	
Current Liabilities			
Bank Overdraft	£820		
Electricity accrued	320		
Bar Creditors	1,900		
'95 Subscriptions in Advance	800	3,840	
Net Current Liabilities			480
			25,840
Accumulated Fund			
Balance at 30 June 1996			26,500
Surplus of Expenditure over Income			−1,200
			25,300
Life Subscriptions [£600 − (£600/10 years)]			540
Balance at 30 June 1997			25,840

W1	Depreciation		'96 NBV	Depreciation	'97 NBV
	Equipment per				
	Note 2	9,300	10%	930	8,370
	Additions	1,500	10%	150	1,350
				1,080	9,720
	New Computer	2,000	20%	400	1,600
	Total Depreciation				
	Charge			1,480	

Section 13

Departmental Accounts

Suggested Solution to Question 13.1

(a)

Ned Ryan
Trading and Profit and Loss Account
for the Year Ended 31 December 1996

	Total		*Building Materials*		*Electrical Goods*	
Sales		£500,000		£300,000		£200,000
Cost of Sales						
Stock on hand on						
1 January	£35,000		£15,000		£20,000	
Purchases	265,000		170,000		95,000	
	300,000		185,000		115,000	
Stock on hand on						
31 December	55,000	245,000	35,000	150,000	20,000	95,000
Gross Profit		255,000		150,000		105,000
Expenses*						
Wages	160,000		96,000		64,000	
Administration						
Costs	12,300		7,380		4,920	
Selling and						
Distribution						
Expenses	7,100		4,260		2,840	
Bank Charges	600		360		240	
Depreciation of						
Premises	1,600		960		640	
Deprec. of Plant						
and Equipment	4,000		2,400		1,600	
Increase in Bad						
Debt Provision	3,000	188,600	1,800	113,160	1,200	75,440
Net Profit		66,400		36,840		29,560

Basis of Apportionment of Expenses

Sales of Building Materials	300,000	= 3/5	or 60%
Sales of Electrical Goods	200,000	= 2/5	or 40%
Total Sales	500,000	= 5/5	or 100%

* Apportionment of Expenses		Building	Electrical
Expense	*Total*	*3/5*	*2/5*
Wages	£160,000	£96,000	£64,000
Administration Costs	12,300	7,380	4,920
Selling and Distribution Expenses	7,100	4,260	2,840
Bank Charges	600	360	240
Depreciation of Premises (80,000 × 2%)	1,600	960	640
Deprec. of Plant and Equipment			
[(£30,000 − £10,000) × 20%]	4,000	2,400	1,600
Increase in Bad Debt Provision			
[(£20,000 × 40%) − £5,000]	3,000	1,800	1,200

Ned Ryan

(b)   Balance Sheet as at 31 December 1996

Fixed Assets	*Cost*	*Depreciation*	*NBV*
Premises	£80,000	£7,600	£72,400
Plant and Equipment	30,000	14,000	16,000
	110,000	21,600	88,400
Current Assets			
Stock		55,000	
Debtors	20,000		
Provision for Bad Debts	−8,000	12,000	
Prepayments		5,000	
		72,000	
Current Liabilities			
Bank Overdraft	15,000		
Creditors and Accruals	18,000	33,000	
Net Current Assets			39,000
Net Assets			127,400
Financed By:			
Capital at the Start of the Year			61,000
Net Profit for the Year			66,400
			127,400

Section 14

Preparation of Final Accounts from Incomplete Records

Suggested Solution to Question 14.1

William Brook
Trading and Profit and Loss Account for the Year Ended 31 December 1996

Sales	W2		£161,000
Cost of Sales			
Opening Stock		Nil	
Purchases	W3	£80,000	
−Closing Stock		−8,000	72,000
Gross Profit			89,000
Administration Costs		45,000	
Selling Expenses		15,000	
Financial Expenses		8,000	68,000
Net Profit			21,000

William Brook
Balance Sheet as at 31 December 1996

Current Assets	
Stock	£8,000
Debtors	24,000
Bank	21,000
	53,000
Current Liabilities	
Trade Creditors	15,000
	38,000
Financed By:	
Capital Introduced	27,000
Profit for the year	21,000
Drawings	−10,000
	38,000

Workings

W1	Receipts from Debtors	
	Lodgements	£164,000
	Capital Introduced	27,000
		137,000

W2   Debtors Control

			Bank (W1)	137,000
Credit Sales				
(derived)	161,000		Balance c/d	24,000
	161,000			161,000

W3   Creditors Control

Bank	65,000			
Balance c/d	15,000		Credit Purchases (derived)	80,000
	80,000			80,000

Suggested Solution to Question 14.2

Mary Lambe
(a)   Profit and Loss Account for the Year Ended 31 December 1996

Sales	W5		£300,000
Cost of Sales			
Opening Stock		£60,000	
Purchases	W1	208,000	
Closing Stock		−40,000	228,000
Gross Profit			72,000
Expenses			
Wages (£40,000 − 8,000 Drawings)		32,000	
Business Expenses	W2	38,000	
Depreciation	W3	12,000	−82,000
Net Loss for the year			10,000

Mary Lambe
(b)   Balance Sheet as at 31 December 1996

Fixed Assets			£108,000
Current Assets			
Stock		£40,000	
Debtors		55,000	
Prepayments		1,000	
		96,000	
Current Liabilities			
Bank	£24,000		
Creditors	14,000		
Accruals	2,000	40,000	56,000
			164,000
Financed By			
Capital at the start of the year	W4		194,000
Loss for the year			−10,000
Drawings (£12,000 cash + £8,000 bank)			−20,000
			164,000

Workings

W1		Creditors Control	
Bank	209,000	Balance b/d	15,000
Balance c/d	14,000	Credit Purchases (derived)	208,000
	223,000		223,000

W2		Expenses	
Balance b/d	2,000	Balance b/d	1,000
Bank	36,000	Profit and Loss	38,000
Balance c/d	2,000	Balance c/d	1,000
	40,000		40,000

W3   Fixed Assets

Net Book Value at 1 January 1996	£100,000
Purchase	20,000
Net Book Value at 31 December 1996	−108,000
Therefore, Depreciation charge for the year	12,000

W4   Capital as at 1 January 1996
Assets

Fixed Assets	£100,000
Stock	60,000
Debtors	50,000
Prepayments	2,000
	212,000

Liabilities

Creditors	£15,000	
Accruals	1,000	
Bank overdraft	2,000	18,000
		194,000

W5		Debtors Control	
Balance b/d	50,000	Bank	283,000
		Drawings	12,000
Credit Sales (derived)	300,000	Balance c/d	55,000
	350,000		350,000

Suggested Solution to Question 14.3

Terry White
(a) Trading, Profit and Loss Account for the Year Ended 31 December 1996

Sales	W2		£128,000
Cost of Sales			
Opening Stock		£22,000	
Purchases		76,000	
Closing Stock		−28,000	70,000
Gross Profit			58,000
Wages		12,000	
Expenses		10,000	22,000
Net Profit			36,000

Terry White
(b)   Balance Sheet as at 31 December 1996

Stock		£28,000
Debtors	W2	26,000
Bank	W1	7,000
		61,000
Creditors	W2	16,000
		45,000
Financed By:		
Capital at the Start of the Year	W3	22,000
Net profit for the Year		36,000
		58,000
Drawings during the Year		13,000
		45,000

Workings

W1   Bank

Balance b/d	2,000	Creditors	80,000
Debtors	120,000	Wages	12,000
		Expenses	10,000
		Capital	13,000
		Balance c/d (derived)	7,000
	122,000		122,000

W2   Debtors

Balance b/d	18,000	Bank	120,000
Credit Sales (derived)	128,000	Balance c/d	26,000
	146,000		146,000

Creditors

Bank	80,000	Balance b/d	20,000
Balance c/d	16,000	Credit Purchases (derived)	76,000
	96,000		96,000

W3   Opening Capital

Assets: (Stock £22,000 + Debtors £18,000 + Bank £2,000)	42,000
Liabilities: Creditors	−20,000
	22,000

Suggested Solution to Question 14.4

Cost of Sales for the year (exclusive of VAT)

Opening Stock (note 5)	£60,000
Purchases (note 4)	520,000
−Closing Stock (note 5)	−80,000
	500,000

Let Cost of Sales from 1 January to 1 July =	x
Then, Cost of Sales from 1 July to 31 December =	1.5x
Cost of Sales for the Full Year	2.5x

But, Cost of Sales for the Full Year (2.5x) = £500,000 (above)
Therefore, x = £200,000 and 1.5x = £300,000

Sales Calculation

	Jan–Jul	Jul–Dec	Total
Gross Margin =	1/3	1/4	
Therefore, Mark-up =	1/2	1/3	
Cost of Sales (above)	£200,000	£300,000	£500,000
Mark-up	100,000	100,000	200,000
Selling Price ex. VAT	300,000	400,000	700,000
VAT charged on sales	45,000	40,000	85,000
Selling Price inc. VAT	345,000	440,000	785,000

Sales for the year (above)	£785,000
Lodgements in respect of sales	635,000
Cash deficiency	150,000

Suggested Solution to Question 14.5

William Greene
Profit and Loss Account for the Year Ended 31 December 1996

Sales		
Sales (net of cash withdrawn)		£200,000
Cash withdrawn (£4,500 × 12)		54,000
		254,000
Cost of Sales		
Opening Stock	Nil	
Cash Purchases (£1,100 × 12)	£13,200	
Credit Purchases (£130,000 − £3,000 refunds)	127,000	
	140,200	
Closing Stock	−12,000	128,200
Gross Profit		125,800
Expenses		
Light and Heat (8,950 − 2,500)	£6,450	
Motor Expenses	17,072	
(18,940 + (12 × £200) − (20% × £21,340))		
Bank Charges	2,800	
Wages [15,400 + (12 × £2,800) + 1,400 Accrual]	50,400	
Rent (15,000 − 3,000 Prepayment)	12,000	
Insurance (9,000 + 3,000 Accrual)	12,000	
Stationery (17,860 − 1,920 stock)	15,940	116,662
Net Profit		9,138

William Greene
Balance Sheet as at 31 December 1996

Current Assets		
Bank (W1)		£15,050
Stock		12,000
Stationery Stock		1,920
Light and Heat Deposit		2,500
Rent Prepaid		3,000
		34,470
Current Liabilities		
PAYE and PRSI Accrual	£1,400	
Insurance Accrual	3,000	4,400
		30,070
Financed By:		
Capital Introduced		30,000
Profit for the year		9,138
Drawings [£4,268 Motor Expenses		
+£4,800 Cash (£400 per month)]		−9,068
		30,070

Workings

W1   Bank

Cash	200,000	Purchases	130,000
Capital	30,000	Light	8,950
Refunds from Creditors	3,000	Print and Stationery	17,860
		Motor Expenses	18,940
		Wages	15,400
		Rent	15,000
		Insurance	9,000
		Bank Charges	2,800
		Balance c/d	15,050
	233,000		233,000

W2		Cash	
Receipts from Sales	254,000	Wages (£2,800 × 12)	33,600
		Drawings (£400 × 12)	4,800
		Purchases (£1,100 × 12)	13,200
		Motor Expenses (£200 × 12)	
		Bank	200,000
	254,000		254,000

Suggested Solution to Question 14.6

George Martin

(a)   Profit and Loss Account for the Year Ended 31 December 1996

Sales (W1)		£353,000
Cost of Sales (W2)		−282,400
Gross Profit (W2)		70,600
Discount received		6,000
		76,600
Expenses		
Light and Heat (£25,000 + £10,000 − £15,000)	£20,000	
Office expenses (£27,000 + £19,000 − £20,000)	26,000	
Bad Debts	4,000	
Discount Allowed	5,000	
Depreciation	4,000	59,000
Net Profit		17,600

George Martin
(b)   Balance Sheet as at 31 December 1996

Fixed Assets			£56,000
Current Assets			
Stock		£30,000	
Debtors		36,000	
Prepayments		15,000	
Bank (W5)		16,100	
		97,100	
Current Liabilities			
Trade Creditors	£50,000		
Accruals	19,000	69,000	28,100
			84,100
Financed By:			
Capital at the Start of the Year			80,000
Profit for the Year			17,600
Drawings during the Year			−13,500
			84,100

W1   Debtors Control

Balance b/d	42,000	Bank	350,000
		Bad Debts	4,000
		Discount Allowed	5,000
Credit Sales (derived)	353,000	Balance c/d	36,000
	395,000		395,000

W2   Cost of Sales
     Gross Profit Mark-up = 1/4;
     Therefore, Gross Profit Margin = 1/5 = 20%

Sales =	£353,000
Therefore, 20% Gross Profit Margin =	70,600
Therefore, Cost of Sales (Sales − Gross Profit) =	282,400

W3   <u>Purchases</u>
Cost of Sales = Opening Stock + Purchases − Closing Stock
Therefore,
Purchases = Cost of Sales + Opening Stock − Closing Stock
= £282,400 − £26,000 + £30,000 = £286,400

W4   Creditors Control

Discount Received	6,000	Balance b/d	48,000
Bank (derived)	278,400		
Balance c/d	50,000	Credit Purchases (W3)	286,400
	334,400		334,400

W5   Bank

Balance b/d	10,000	Light and Heat	25,000
		Expenses	27,000
		Capital	13,500
		Creditors (W4)	278,400
Debtors	350,000	Balance c/d	16,100
	360,000		360,000

Suggested Solution to Question 14.7

Brian Ward
(a)   Profit and Loss Account for the Year Ended 31 December 1996

Sales (£4,714 + £360 not yet invoiced)		£5,074
Expenses		
Accountancy fees	£100	
Repairs	572	
Insurance	245	
Petrol	416	
Bank charges	95	
Depreciation (£6,500 over 5 years)	1,300	2,728
Net Profit		2,346

Brian Ward
(b)   Balance Sheet as at 31 December 1996

Fixed Assets (£6,500 − £1,300 depreciation)			£5,200
Current Assets			
Debtors (sales not yet invoiced)		£360	
Current Liabilities			
Bank (W1 and W2)	£2,698		
Accountancy Fee Accrual	100	2,798	−2,438
			2,762
Financed By:			
Capital Introduced			10,000
Profit for the Year			2,346
			12,346
Drawings (W1)			9,584
			2,762

Workings

W1   Bank

Capital	£10,000	Fixed Asset	£6,500
Debtors	4,714	*Cheques*	
		Repairs	572
		Insurance	245
		Petrol etc.	416
		Charges	95
Balance c/d (W2)	2,698	Drawings (derived)	9,584
	17,412		17,412

W2   Bank Reconciliation Statement

Balance per Bank Statement (overdraft)	£2,498
Outstanding Cheque	200
Balance per Bank Account in Nominal Ledger (credit)	2,698

Suggested Solution to Question 14.8

(a)(i)   Bank

Jan 1	Capital	£12,000			Creditors	£27,000
	Debtors	48,000			Expenses and Rent	20,000
					Drawings	6,000
			Dec 31		Balance c/d	7,000
		60,000				60,000

Joe Singleton
(a)(ii)   Trading and Profit and Loss Account
for the Year Ended 31 December 1996

Sales		£50,000
Cost of Sales		
Opening Stock	Nil	
Purchases	£30,000	
Closing Stock	−4,000	26,000
Gross Profit		24,000
Expenses		20,000
Net Profit		4,000

Joe Singleton
(a)(iii)   Balance Sheet as at 31 December 1996

Current Assets	
Stock	£4,000
Debtors (W1)	2,000
Bank	7,000
	13,000
Current Liabilities	
Creditors (W2)	3,000
	10,000
Financed By:	
Capital Introduced	12,000
Profit for the Year	4,000
Drawings	−6,000
	10,000

Workings

W1   Debtors Control

	Sales (Credit)	50,000		Bank	48,000
		50,000	Dec 31	Balance c/d	2,000
					50,000

W2   Creditors Control

	Bank	27,000		
Dec 31	Balance c/d	3,000	Purchases (Credit)	30,000
		30,000		30,000

(b) The reasons why the balance per the bank account in Joe Singleton's accounting records might be different from the bank balance according to the Statement from his bank at the same date can be divided into two:

(i) Errors in the bank account or on the Bank Statements, and

(ii) Differences due to the timing of entries made by the bank or the business. Errors in the bank account or on the Bank Statements could be:

    (a) Errors made by the bank, such as a cheque for another customer charged in Joe's account:

    (b) Errors made by the business, such as a receipt or payment entered as the wrong amount.

Differences arising due to the timing of entries made by the bank or the business could be:

    (a) Outstanding cheques: i.e. cheques entered in the bank account as paid but not yet presented to the bank.

    (b) Outstanding lodgements: i.e. lodgements made to the bank and entered in the bank account but not yet processed by the bank:

    (c) Items, payments or receipts initiated by the bank and on the Bank Statements but not yet put through the bank account.

Suggested Solution to Question 14.9

Cost of Sales for the period 1 January to 31 December

Opening Stock (per note 4)	£94,500
+ Purchases (per note 1)	296,750
− Closing Stock*	109,250
	282,000

*£106,600 per note 4 + goods stolen £2,650 per note 5

Sales (per note 2)	£376,000
Cost of Sales (above)	282,000
Therefore, Gross Profit	94,000

Mark-up = GP/Cost of Sales = £94,000/£282,000 = $33\frac{1}{3}$%
Margin = GP/Sales = £94,000/£376,000 = 25%
Cost of Sales = Opening Stock + Purchases − Closing Stock
Therefore, Closing Stock = Opening Stock + Purchases − Cost of Sales
But, Closing Stock = Cost of Stock Destroyed
Therefore, Cost of Stock Destroyed =

Opening Stock (4)	£106,600
+ Purchases (1)	102,250
	208,850

−Cost of Sales for the period 1 January to 25 April		
Sales and Cash Stolen (£127,300 + £500)	£127,800	
Less Gross Profit (25% of Sales for the period)	31,950	95,850
		113,000

Suggested Solution to Question 14.10

(a)   Cash

Balance b/d	900	Creditors	1,800
Debtors	83,555	Bank Lodgements (derived)	81,503
Bad debts recovered	48	Balance c/d	1,200
	84,503		84,503

Debtors Control

Balance b/d	£8,027	Cash	£83,555
		Bad Debts	760
		Discount allowed	612
Credit Sales (derived)	87,900	Balance c/d	11,000
	95,927		95,927

Creditors Control

Bank	£59,126	Balance b/d	£6,492
Cash	1,800		
Discount Received	641		
Balance c/d	4,925	Credit Purchases (derived)	60,000
	66,492		66,492

(b)   Sales – Cost of Sales = Gross Profit
      Therefore, Sales – Gross Profit = Cost of Sales

	A	B	Total
Total Sales			£87,900
Sales by Category	70%	30%	100%
	£61,530	£26,370	£87,900
Percentage Mark-up	25%	$33\frac{1}{3}\%$	
Therefore, Percentage Margin	20%	25%	
Value of Margin (% × Sales Value)	£12,306	£6,593	
Cost of Sales (COS)			
(Sales – Margin Value)	£49,224	£19,777	
Opening Stock (O)	£16,843	£8,106	
Purchases (P)	£42,000	£18,000	£60,000
Therefore, Closing Stock (11 August)			
(P + O – COS)	£9,619	£6,329	£15,948

Cost of Goods Destroyed by the Fire = Closing Stock (11 August) = £15,948

Suggested Solution to Question 14.11

Alan Strong
(a)   Statement of Affairs as at 1 January 1996

Fixed Asset			
Premises (note 2)			£25,000
Current Assets			
Stock (note 1)		£6,300	
Debtors (note 1)		4,100	
Prepayments (note 1)		400	
		10,800	
Current Liabilities			
Trade Creditors (note 1)	£ 3,900		
Accruals (£500 wages and salaries			
+ £200 rates)	700		
Bank Overdraft (per bank account)	2,016	6,616	4,184
			29,184
Financed by:			
Capital (to balance)			29,184
(= assets − liabilities)			

(b)

Alan Strong
Trading and Profit and Loss Account
for the Year Ended 31 December 1996

Sales	W1		£89,900
Cost of Sales			
Opening Stock (note 1)		£6,300	
Purchases	W2	44,200	
Closing Stock (note 1)		8,400	42,100
Gross Profit			47,800
Deposit Interest earned (note 3)			400
			48,200
Expenses			
Wages and Salaries (£8,100 + £750 − £500)		£8,350	
Rent and Rates (£1,250 + £300 − £200)		1,350	
Light and Heat (£3,200 + £400 − £300)		3,300	
Printing and Stationery		2,300	
Telephone		1,100	
General Expenses (£4,300 + £800 cash)		5,100	
Depreciation [(Van £6,500 × 10%)			
+ £2,500 on premises]		3,150	24,650
Net Profit			23,550

Alan Strong
(c)   Balance Sheet as at 31 December 1996

Fixed Assets			
Premises (new valuation)			£22,500
Van (£6,500 − £650 depreciation for the year)			5,850
			28,350
Current Assets			
Stock		£8,400	
Debtors		4,600	
Prepayments		300	
Bank Deposit Account			
(including £400 Interest earned)		5,400	
Bank Current Account (reconciled)		7,334	
		26,034	
Current Liabilities			
Trade Creditors	£4,200		
Accruals (£750 wages and salaries			
+ £300 rates)	1,050	5,250	20,784
			49,134
Financed by:			
Capital at the start of the year [per part (a)]			29,184
Net Profit			23,550
Drawings (note 5)			−3,600
			49,134

W1   Debtors Control

Balance b/d	£4,100	Lodged	£84,000
		Not Lodged	
		(800 + 1,000 + 3,600)	5,400
Credit Sales	89,900	Balance c/d	4,600
	94,000		94,000

W2   Creditors Control

Payments	£42,900	Balance b/d	£3,900
Cash	1,000	Credit Purchases	44,200
Balance c/d	4,200		
	48,100		48,100

Suggested Solution to Question 14.12

John Wells
Profit and Loss Account for the Period Ended 28 March 1997

Sales (£142,969 on Credit (W2) + £17,481 for Cash + £160 Cash Destroyed)			£160,610
Cost of Sales			
Opening Stock		Nil	
Purchases [£2,300 cash + £108,450 credit (W3)]		£110,750	
Closing Stock (£4,500 in Van + £7,800 destroyed)		−12,300	98,450
Gross Profit			62,160
Expenses			
Bad Debts		£804	
Cash Discount		2,405	
Wages	W4	26,600	
Other Expenses			
(£450 cash + £1,800 bank + £120 due)		2,370	
Loss on Disposal of Van			
(£7,500 NBV − £6,800 proceeds)		700	
Rent (£4,800 × 7/12)		2,800	
Depreciation (20% of £22,000)		4,400	40,079
Net Profit			22,081

John Wells
Balance Sheet as at 28 March 1997

Fixed Asset
Van [£22,000 cost – 20% depreciation (total = current year)]   £17,600

Current Assets
Stock		£4,500
Bank	W1	15,806
Insurance Claim Receivable		14,760
(£7,800 + £6,800 + £160)		
Trade Debtors		11,500
		46,566

Current Liabilities
Trade Creditors	£10,090	
Wages Accrued	2,250	
PAYE Accrued	625	
Expense Creditors Accrued	120	
Rent Accrued (£4,800 p.a.		
× 7 months – £2,400 paid)	400	13,485

Net Current Assets	33,081
	50,681
Long-term Loan [£30,000	−25,000
received – £5,000 repaid (all capital)]	
Net Assets	25,681

Financed By:
Capital Introduced	12,000
Drawings (£7,420 bank + £980 cash expenses)	−8,400
Profit for the Year	22,081
	25,681

W1
Bank

Debtors	£125,500	Wages	£21,425
Wages – grants received	1,800	Drawings	7,420
Capital	12,000	Creditors	95,600
Cash Sales	17,481	Cash expenses	4,080
Loan	30,000	Expense Creditors	1,800
		Wages – PAYE	3,750
		Office Equipment	7,500
		Van	22,000
		Loan	5,000
		Rent	2,400
		Balance c/d	15,806
	186,781		186,781

W2
Debtors Control

		Bank	£125,500
		Bad Debts	804
		Cash Discount	2,405
		Creditors	2,760
Credit Sales (derived)	142,969	Balance c/d	11,500
	142,969		142,969

W3   Credit Purchases = £95,600 paid + £2,760 offset + £10,090 closing
creditors. bal. = £108,450

W4
Wages

Bank (£21,425 + £3,750)	£25,175	Bank – training grants	£1,800
Accruals (£2,250 + £625)	2,875		
Cash Expenses	350	Profit and Loss	26,600
	28,400		28,400

W5
Rent

Bank	2,400		
Balance c/d – Accrual	400	Profit and Loss (£4,800 × 7/12)	2,800
	2,800		2,800

Suggested Solution to Question 14.13

Ben Lewis
Profit and Loss Account for the Year Ended 31 March 1997

Sales			
Credit Sales (from Debtors Control)			£66,900
Cash Sales (see Cash account)			30,600
			97,500
Cost of Sales			
Opening Stock		£16,000	
Purchases (from Creditors Control)		58,200	
Closing Stock		−18,400	−55,800
Gross Profit			41,700
Profit on sale of plant	W2		250
Discount Received			2,100
			44,050
Wages and expenses (£11,100 Bank + £9,400 Cash)		£20,500	
Bad Debts		3,000	
Provision for legal claim (£6,400 paid − £5,000 already provided)		1,400	
Discount Allowed		1,200	
Depreciation [(£9,000 + £14,000) × 25% + (£40,000 × 5%)]		7,750	33,850
Net Profit			10,200

Ben Lewis
Balance Sheet as at 31 March 1997

Fixed Assets			
Plant [(£18,000 + £14,000 additions − £9,000			
disposal) − £8,000 depreciation]	W2		£15,000
Premises (£40,000 − £4,000 depreciation)	W2		36,000
			51,000
Current Assets			
Stock		£18,400	
Debtors	W3	15,700	
Bank	W1	1,400	
Cash (per note 4)		400	
		35,900	
Current Liabilities			
Trade Creditors	W3	16,100	
Net Current Assets			19,800
Net Assets			70,800
Financed By:			
Capital at the start of the year			62,000
Profit for the year			10,200
New Capital Introduced (Inheritance)			12,000
Drawings (Bank)			−13,400
			70,800

Workings

W1   Bank

Apr 1	Balance b/d	3,000	Mar 31	Creditors – Payments	58,000
Mar 31	Fixed Assets Disposal	2,000	Mar 31	Fixed Assets –	
				Purchases	14,000
Mar 31	Debtors – receipts	64,000	Mar 31	Wages and Expenses	11,100
Mar 31	Cash – Lodgements	27,000	Mar 31	Legal Claim	6,400
Mar 31	Insurance Proceeds	5,000	Mar 31	Cash	5,700
			Mar 31	Drawings	13,400
			Mar 31	Debtors – Bad debt	3,000
	Capital – Inheritance	12,000	Mar 31	Balance c/d	1,400
		113,000			113,000

W2   Plant (at Cost)

Apr 1	Balance b/d	18,000	Mar 31	Disposal of Plant	9,000
Mar 31	Bank (Additions)	14,000	Mar 31	Balance c/d	23,000
		32,000			32,000

Disposal of Plant

Mar 31	Plant at Cost	£9,000	Mar 31	Bank (insurance)	£5,000
				Bank (scrap)	2,000
				Prov. for Deprec.	
	Profit and Loss	250		(£9k × 25%)	2,250
		9,250			9,250

Provision for Depreciation on Plant

Mar 31	Disposal	£2,250	Apr 1	Balance b/d	£4,500
			Mar 31	P&L ((£9,000	
Mar 31	Balance c/d	8,000		+£14,000) × 25%)	5,750
		10,250			10,250

Provision for Depreciation on Premises

			Apr 1	Balance b/d	2,000
Mar 31	Balance c/d	4,000	Mar 31	P&L (£40,000 × 5%)	2,000
		4,000			4,000

W3   Debtors Control

Apr 1	Balance b/d	£14,000	Mar 31	Bank	£64,000
Mar 31	Dishonoured Cheque	3,000	Mar 31	Bad Debts	3,000
			Mar 31	Discount Allowed	1,200
Mar 31	Credit Sales (derived)	66,900	Mar 31	Balance c/d	15,700
		83,900			83,900

Creditors Control

Mar 31	Bank	£58,000	Apr 1	Balance b/d	£18,000
Mar 31	Discount Received	2,100			
			Mar 31	Credit Purchases	
Mar 31	Balance c/d	16,100		(derived)	58,200
		76,200			76,200

Cash

Apr 1	Balance b/d	500	Mar 31	Wages and Expenses	9,400
Mar 31	Bank	5,700	Mar 31	Bank – Lodgements	27,000
Mar 31	Cash Sales (derived)	30,600	Mar 31	Balance c/d	400
		36,800			36,800

Section 15

Ratio Analysis

Suggested Solution to Question 15.1

Some Limitations of Ratio Analysis

1. Accounting statements present only a limited picture of a business. The information covered in accounts does not cover all aspects of the business.
2. The accounts of large organisations frequently aggregate operations in different industries. An external analysis therefore will not be able to split up the results of one sector from another.
3. Differing bases of accounting present many problems in relation to ratio analysis. In particular, differences in the valuation of fixed assets, depreciation methods and in valuation of stock can be mentioned. Such a variety of accounting methods may render inter-firm or inter-industry comparisons invalid.
4. Comparison of a firm which finances its fixed plant through rental, thus not showing it as an asset, with a firm which purchases its own assets, will be difficult.
5. External analysis of balances can be misleading because the picture at that particular moment of time may not be representative of the year as a whole.
6. Interpretation of a change in any ratio needs careful examination of changes in both numerator and denominator. Without a very full and detailed investigation some wrong conclusions may be drawn.

7. There is room for considerable difference between individual companies. It is not wise to lay down very rigid guidelines, since what may be good for one successful firm, may not be for another.

8. Since many of the general industrial analyses of ratios are overall averages, they may not be appropriate as comparisons between a small and a large firm.

Suggested Solution to Question 15.2

(a) Return on Capital Employed   *Net Profit (after tax)/Total Assets*
Return on capital employed shows the overall performance of the company, indicating how successfully management has used the Net Assets of the company to generate Income or Profit. It measures the overall return on investment from operations.

(b) Net Profit Margin   *Net Profit (after tax)/Sales*
This ratio, also known as Net Margin, measures the overall profitability of the firm's trading. More specifically it indicates by how much the profit margin can decline before the firm makes losses.

(c) Stock Turnover   *Cost of Sales/Average Stock*
This ratio measures the rate of stock turnover; how many times the firm turns over stock in a given period of time. The quicker stock is sold, the more profit will be made, provided that the gross profit margin does not decline.

(d) Current Ratio   *Current Assets: Current Liabilities*
This ratio gives an indication of the short-term liquidity position of the firm. In general terms it compares assets which will become liquid within approximately twelve months, with liabilities which will be due for payment in the same period. More specifically, it indicates whether the firm has a sufficiently large amount of current assets to cover liabilities and the eventuality of losses.

(e) Acid-Test Ratio   *Current Assets less Stock: Current Liabilities*
This ratio measures the immediate to short-term liquidity position of the firm. It takes into account only those current assets which are cash or will convert very quickly into cash. It is based on the assumption that stock will not be converted into cash quickly enough to meet the time scale for the payment of creditors. It therefore shows that, provided creditors and debtors are paid at approximately the same time, the company has sufficient liquid resources to meet its current liabilities.

(f) Average Collection Period for Debtors
                    Debtors × 365/Credit Sales (Answer in Days)
This ratio tells us the average time taken to turn debtors into cash. A long period of credit shows signs of weakness because it indicates that more money is 'tied up' in debtors. The credit period should be compared to firms in a similar industry.

Suggested Solution to Question 15.3

(a) (i)   Stock Turnover Rate = Cost of Sales/Average Stock

Cost of Sales		Average Stock	
Opening Stock	£30,000	Opening Stock	£30,000
+Purchases	100,000	Closing Stock	50,000
−Closing Stock	50,000		80,000
	80,000	Average = £80,000/2 =	40,000

Stock Turnover = £80,000/£40,000 = 2 times

(ii) Current Ratio = Current Assets : Current Liabilities

Current Assets		Current Liabilities	
Bank	£6,000	Creditors	£30,000
Debtors	25,000	Accruals	10,000
Stock	50,000	Short-Term Bank Loan	14,000
	81,000		54,000

Current Ratio = £81,000 : £54,000 = 1.5 : 1

(iii) Acid-Test Ratio = (Current Assets − Stock) : Current Liabilities
= (£81,000 − £50,000) : £54,000 = 0.57 : 1

(b) *Significance of the rate of Stock Turnover*
This ratio means the number of times, on average, that the stock has 'turned over' (been replaced) during the year. Turnover rate can be high or low, depending on the state of the firm and practice in the industry. For example, stock turnover would be high in supermarkets and relatively low in a jewellery shop. When the rate of stock turnover is falling it can be due to such causes as a slowing down of sales activity, or to keeping a higher amount of stock than is really necessary.

It is important to note that the ratio does not prove anything by itself, it merely prompts inquiries as to why it should be changing.

Suggested Solution to Question 15.4

(1) *Gross Profit Margin*
 = (Gross Profit * 100)/Sales
 Year Ended 31 March 1995: £152,900 * 100/£505,000 = 30.3%
 Year Ended 31 March 1996: £172,750 * 100/£385,000 = 44.9%
 The ratio has increased from 30.3% to 44.9%. Possible explanations are:
 (i) Changes in the types of goods sold, where some lines carry different rates of gross profit than others.
 (ii) Increase in the selling price of goods without a proportionate increase in the cost price.
 (iii) Elimination of inefficiencies and factors such as theft which would reduce the profit margin.

(2) *Stock Turnover*
 = Cost of Sales/Average Stock (Cost of Sales = Sales less Gross Profit)
 Year Ended 31 March 1995: £352,100/£84,000 = 4.2 times
 Year Ended 31 March 1996: £212,250/£85,000 = 2.5 times
 In the first year the average stock was turned over 4.2 times. This has deteriorated to 2.5 times in the second year. This has happened because although sales and purchases have fallen considerably, stock levels have remained relatively constant. It may well be possible to reduce stock levels if this reduction is likely to be permanent.

(3) *Current Ratio*
 = Current Assets : Current Liabilities
 As at 31 March 1995: £180,000 : £174,000 = 1.04 : 1
 As at 31 March 1996: £142,000 : £59,000 = 2.41 : 1
 Current Assets were roughly equal to Current Liabilities at 31 March 1995. However, Mr. Giles might have difficulty paying his liabilities on time, depending on how quickly his current assets could be turned into cash. His position at 31 March 1996 appears comfortable, with Current Assets equal to 2.41 times Current Liabilities.

(4) *Acid-test Ratio*
 = (Current Assets less Stock) : Current Liabilities
 As at 31 March 1995: £94,000 : £174,000 = 0.54 : 1
 As at 31 March 1996: £58,000 : £59,000 = 0.98 : 1
 At 31 March 1995 quick assets (those readily convertible into cash) amount to only 54% of current liabilities. If the current liabilities are required to be paid promptly Mr. Giles would not be able to meet these in full. At 31 March 1996, quick assets approximately equalled current liabilities, and he should then have been in a position to meet the total liabilities.

(5) *Period of Credit Given*
 =   (Debtors * 365)/Sales
       Year Ended 31 March 1995: (£94,000 * 365)/£505,000 = 68 days
       Year Ended 31 March 1996: (£58,000 * 365)/£385,000 = 55 days
The average period of credit given to customers has decreased from 68 days
to 55 days. This ratio reflects the time taken by customers to pay and should
approximate to the credit terms allowed by the business. The situation has
improved and, viewed in conjunction with the fall in sales, this would suggest
that Mr. Giles has been more selective in deciding to whom he sells goods on
credit.

Suggested Solution to Question 15.5

(a) (i)   Current Ratio
               = Current Assets : Current Liabilities
               = £213,000 : £48,000
               = 4.44 : 1
      (ii)   Acid-Test Ratio
               = (Current Assets less Stock) : Current Liabilities
               = (£213,000 − £120,000) : £48,000
               = 1.94 : 1
      (iii) Stock Turnover
               = Cost of Sales/Average Stock
               = £270,000/[(£80,000 + £120,000)/2]
               = 2.7 times
      (iv) Period of Credit Given to Debtors
               = (£55,000/£400,000) × 365 days
               = 50 days
(b) Comment on Period of Credit Given to Debtors
      The above ratio is an important analysis tool because it shows the resources
      which are tied up in debtors, and gives an average figure of how long it will
      take for such cash to be released.

      In the case of Ted Sharp, debtors are taking approximately 50 days to pay.

Suggested Solution to Question 15.6

(a) *Gross Profit Margin*
 = (Gross Profit * 100)/Sales
  Year Ended 31 March 1996 = (£122,500 × 100)/£350,000 = 35%
  Year Ended 31 March 1997 = (£92,000 × 100)/£460,000 = 20%
 The rate of gross profit achieved in the second year shows a substantial deterioration compared to that achieved in the first year. Possible explanations would include:
 (i) Price cutting to boost or maintain sales levels.
 (ii) Changes in the type of goods sold where some lines carry different rates of gross profit than others.
 (iii) Theft.
 (iv) Increase in the cost of sales without a proportionate increase in the selling price.
 The deterioration is very substantial and unless it was brought about by a deliberate policy of management, for example drastically reducing sales price in the short-term in order to compete with a rival firm, it would warrant detailed examination.

(b) *Stock Turnover*
 = Cost of Sales/Average Stock
  Cost of Sales = Sales − Gross Profit
   Year Ended 31 March 1996 = £350,000 − £122,500 = £227,500
   Year Ended 31 March 1997 = £460,000 − £92,000 = £368,000
  Average Stock = (Opening Stock + Closing Stock)/2
   Year Ended 31 March 1996 = (£52,500 + £54,500)/2 = £53,500
   Year Ended 31 March 1997 = (£54,500 + £80,700)/2 = £67,600
  Stock Turnover
  Year Ended 31 March 1996 = £227,500/£53,500 = 4.25 times
  Year Ended 31 March 1997 = £368,000/£67,600 = 5.44 times
 In the first year the average stock was turned over 4.25 times. In the second year this improved to 5.44 times. A possible cause for the increase is an increase in sales activity, perhaps due to the lowering of the gross profit margin seen above.

(c) *Current Ratio*
 = Current Assets : Current Liabilities
  As at 31 March 1996 = £109,700 : £55,000 = 2 : 1 (approx.)
  As at 31 March 1997 = £160,200 : £160,000 = 1 : 1 (approx.)
 Mr. Parker's current assets were approximately equal to his current liabilities at 31 March 1997. However, he might have difficulty paying his liabilities on time, depending on how quickly his current assets could be converted into cash. The position at 31 March 1996, with current assets equal to twice current liabilities, appeared adequate.

(d) *Acid-Test Ratio*
   = (Current Assets excluding Stock) : Current Liabilities
     As at 31 March 1996 = £55,200 : £55,000 = 1 : 1 (approx.)
     As at 31 March 1997 = £80,700 : £160,000 = 0.5 : 1 (approx.)

The position at 31 March 1997 shows that assets readily convertible into cash amount to only half of the current liabilities. If the current liabilities are required to be paid promptly Mr. Parker would not be able to meet these in full. At 31 March 1996, the quick assets approximately equalled current liabilities, and he should then have been in a position to meet the total liabilities.

(e) *Period of Credit Given*
   = (Debtors × 365/Sales)
     Year Ended 31 March 1996 = (£55,200 × 365)/£350,000 = 58 days
     Year Ended 31 March 1997 = (£80,700 × 365)/£460,000 = 64 days

The Period of Credit Given to debtors has increased from 58 days to 64 days.

This ratio reflects the time taken by debtors to pay and should approximate to the credit terms allowed by the business. Better terms may have been given to customers in order to boost sales. However, if the increase has not been dictated by management, steps should be taken to restore the sanctioned credit period.

Suggested Solution to Question 15.7

(a) (i)   *Gross Profit Margin* = Gross Profit × 100/Sales
           Small Electrical Goods: = 8,000 × 100/30,000 = 26.67%
           Large Electrical Goods: = 8,000 × 100/70,000 = 11.43%
     (ii) *Stock Turnover* = Cost of Sales/Average Stock
           Small Electrical Goods: = 22,000/[(4,000 + 6,000)/2] = 4.4 times
           Large Electrical Goods: = 62,000/[(10,000 + 8,000)/2] = 6.89 times
     (iii) *Current Ratio* = Current Assets : Current Liabilities
           = 32,000 : 40,000 = 0.8 : 1
     (iv) *Acid-Test Ratio* = (Current Assets less Stock) : Current Liabilities
           = (32,000 − 14,000) : 40,000 = 0.45 : 1
     (v)   *Debtors Days Outstanding* = Trade Debtors × 365/Credit Sales
           = 18,000 × 365/100,000 = 65.7 Days
           It is assumed that 'Debtors' includes only Trade Debtors and that all sales are on credit.
     (vi) *Creditors Days Outstanding* = Trade Creditors × 365/Credit Purchases
           = 12,000 × 365/84,000 = 52.14 Days
           It is assumed that all purchases are on credit.

(b) Appliances Ltd has a very poor liquidity position at present. Its current ratio is only 0.8 : 1. This indicates that the company may not be able to meet its short-term financial obligations.

The acid-test ratio, at 0.45 : 1, is also quite low. This ratio attempts to eliminate some of the disadvantages of the current ratio by concentrating on strictly liquid assets. It is based on the assumption that stock will not be converted into cash quickly enough in order to pay creditors. It is obvious here that Appliances Ltd. does not have sufficient liquid assets to pay its immediate short-term liabilities.

If the company was to come under short-term pressure from creditors (including VAT due and the bank overdraft), it would have difficulty in paying them even if it collected all of its debtors very quickly. If some of the company's sales were for cash this would help the situation, as it would be able to convert stock into cash without first converting them into debtors, and then waiting an average of 65.7 days to receive cash. At a minimum, the company will have to pay its VAT liability and at least some of its trade creditors within the next month, and may require additional financing in order to do so if it has already used all of its overdraft facility.

The long-term liquidity position of Appliances Ltd is also quite poor. It is financed by a Long-term Loan which is more than the net assets of the business. Repayments of the interest on, and the principal amount of, this loan will reduce the firm's ability to pay its other commitments in the short-term.

In terms of gearing (in this case Long-term Loan/Ordinary Share Capital + Revenue Reserves + Long-term Loan) it can be seen that the long-term loan represents 52.7% of the company's total financing, thereby exceeding the shareholders' funds. This level of gearing is not necessarily a problem, but in this case, coupled with the poor short-term liquidity position, needs to be addressed urgently. It would be inadvisable, and probably not possible, for the company to raise more loans.

(c) From the ratios calculated above, it can be seen that the average number of debtors days outstanding is 65.7 days. The rate of stock turnover during the period is 4.4 times and 6.9 times for Small and Large electrical goods respectively. This low rate of stock turnover, coupled with a long period of credit given to debtors, indicates that a large amount of money is tied up in Working Capital. The company should take steps to increase its rate of stock turnover and to tighten its credit policy in order to release funds to finance current and long-term liabilities.

The company would also benefit from an injection of share capital.

Ultimately, the company needs to improve profitability. As the electrical business is competitive, it may not be possible to raise prices without a large fall in sales volume. Therefore, profitability must be improved by reducing costs and/or changing the sales mix in favour of 'small' electrical goods, which generate a gross margin of 26.27% compared with only 11.43% from 'large' electrical goods.

Suggested Solution to Question 15.8

The Managing Director Date
Soda Ltd.

Dear Mr. X,

Comparison of your Company with Tonic Ltd. for 1996

I refer to your letter requesting a comparison of the results of your company with Tonic Ltd. for 1996.

For convenience I have attached an addendum listing comparative performance indicators to which I will refer below. I have collated these indicators under the headings of Profitability Ratios, Liquidity Ratios, Working Capital Ratios, Asset Performance Ratios and Gearing Ratios.

In interpreting these performance indicators, it is necessary to exercise a degree of caution and not concentrate on one specific ratio as that may give a misleading picture, but examine all the indicators and be alert to those which arouse anxiety.

The Profitability Ratios indicate that Tonic is outperforming Soda in all areas. Soda's gross profit margin of 55.7% is 1.7% less than Tonic's (57.4%), and has been translated into a decrease of 2.9% in the profit margin before interest on debentures is charged. This reflects Tonic's lower figure for expenses, 25.9% of sales as against Soda's 27.1%. There is cause for reflection on this as while Soda's turnover is almost 30% higher than Tonic's, this increase has not given rise to economies of scale either in cost of goods sold or expenses.

After charging debenture interest, Soda's net profit to sales percentage has fallen by 4.9% compared with Tonic's. This further fall of 2% is due to Soda's debenture interest being 5.7% of sales, while Tonic's is 3.7%. All these combine to reflect only a 6.7% increase in Soda's profit figures over Tonic's, despite an increase of 29.6% in sales value.

The return on Capital Employed shows a marked increase for Tonic over that for Soda; whether looked at from the viewpoint of gross capital employed (adjusting for both debentures and debenture interest) or only the shareholders' funds, the difference is very substantial. In the first situation, Soda's profit percentage shows a fall of 16.5% and in the second 21.8%. The higher return being achieved by Tonic may mean that its shares will command a higher price than Soda's shares if a sale is ever contemplated.

Looking at the financing of both companies, on the surface, Soda's liquidity ratios are much stronger than Tonic's. The current ratio of Soda is 2.6 : 1 while that of Tonic is 1.8 : 1; the 'acid-test' is 1.6 : 1 for Soda and 1.1 : 1 for Tonic. At the Balance Sheet date, both companies have strong working capital and neither have had recourse to bank borrowing. Indeed, Soda is in a stronger position than Tonic as it has money in the bank and can self finance any immediate cash requirement; Tonic would need bank assistance. This, however, is the only area where Soda shows better ratios than Tonic, but may indicate that Soda has excessive current assets or even has overvalued some of these assets.

The analysis of working capital shows that Soda's performance is generally less satisfactory than that of Tonic. The sales/debtors ratio shows that while Soda grants an average of 67 days credit, Tonic grants only 45 days credit. This may, of course, reflect a different bad debt write off policy and you should look at this, also considering whether Soda's sales increase is achieved at a greater risk of bad debt. As a corollary of this, Soda's debtors as a percentage of current assets are 56% against 60% for Tonic and, if the bank balance is excluded, Soda's debtors fall to 41% against 60% for Tonic. This ratio needs to be considered in conjunction with the rate of stock turnover. Soda's stock turnover (measured against sales) is 8.75 times against 13.5 times for Tonic. This is a considerable difference, and thus Soda's stock policy should be examined to see where it can be improved. Consideration may have to be given to establishing whether any of Soda's stock is obsolete and requires to be written off. Taking the total current assets, the performance of Soda is again inferior to that of Tonic. Soda turns over its current assets 3.41 times while Tonic manages 5.4 times. Working Capital is turned over 5.6 times by Soda but 12 times by Tonic. Clearly this area requires examining as there seems to be substantial room for improvement by Soda.

Looking at the Fixed Asset Performance, Soda's performance is below that of Tonic. Fixed Assets are turned over 1.52 times by Soda and 1.86 times by Tonic. The comparability of these ratios depends on the accuracy of the Fixed Asset valuations and whether recent valuations have been made. In considering the Fixed Assets/Total Assets ratio, Soda has 69% invested in Fixed Assets while Tonic has 74%. Soda has proportionately less of an investment in Fixed Assets than Tonic, yet Tonic has been able to turn over its increased investment 1.86 times as against Soda's 1.52 times. This may point to an under-utilisation of fixed assets by Soda.

The fixed asset adverse ratio is carried on to the net assets, as Soda's net assets turnover is 1.20 times against 1.61 times by Tonic. Clearly action is necessary to reduce the competitive advantage that Tonic has over Soda, by increasing the efficiency of asset utilisation.

In its capital structure Soda is more highly geared than Tonic, 66.7% against 52.3%. This is not a serious matter as both companies would not be classed as highly geared, and thus in a potentially dangerous financial position if their profitability deteriorated. The interest cover on debt is high in both companies although it is 3.5 times higher in Tonic than in Soda. An interest cover of 5 times, as in Soda's case, would not cause a lender any worry and would provide a margin for further borrowing should the necessity arise.

I hope that the foregoing enables you to gauge how Soda is performing in relation to Tonic, and directs you to those areas of Soda which can be improved. In conclusion, I would point out that I have assumed that the two companies are comparable in operating terms and my findings are based on that assumption.

Should you need any further information I will be glad to be of assistance.

Yours sincerely,

Addendum

Profitability Ratios	SODA	TONIC
Profit Margins		
Gross Profit/Sales	55.7%	57.4%
Profit before Debenture Interest/Sales	28.6%	31.5%
Net Profit/Sales	22.9%	27.8%
Expenses Ratios		
Cost of Sales/Sales	44.3%	42.6%
Expenses (excl. Debenture Interest)/Sales	27.1%	25.9%
Debenture Interest/Sales	5.7%	3.7%
Return on Capital		
Profit before interest/Capital Employed (including debentures)	34.2%	50.7%
Profit after interest/Shareholders' funds (equity)	46.4%	68.2%
Liquidity Ratios		
Current Ratio	2.6 : 1	1.8 : 1
Acid-Test	1.6 : 1	1.1 : 1
Working Capital Ratios		
Sales/Debtors	67 days	45 days
Debtors/Current Assets	56%	60%
Debtors/Current Assets, less Bank	41%	60%
Sales/Current Assets	3.4 times	5.4 times
Sales/Working Capital (CA − CL)	5.6 times	12 times
Stock Turnover* (Sales/Stock)	8.75 times	13.5 times

*This is an approximation as sales is used in the absence of cost of materials consumed. However, as both ratios are prepared on the same basis, comparison is possible.

Asset Performance Ratios
Asset Turnover

Sales/Fixed Assets	1.52 times	1.86 times
Sales/Net Assets	1.20 times	1.61 times

Fixed Asset Investment

Fixed Assets/Total Assets Employed	69%	74%

Gearing Ratios

Debentures less bank balance/Shareholders Funds	66.7%	52.3%
Interest Cover (Debenture Interest/Profit and Interest)	5 times	8.5 times

Suggested Solution to Question 15.9

(a)   Profit Statement

Sales			£100,000
Cost of Sales			−60,000
Gross Profit	(40% of Sales)		40,000
Expenses			
Selling Expenses	(14% of Sales)	£14,000	
Administration Costs		12,000	
Interest on Long-Term Debt	(£35,000 @ 10%)	3,500	29,500
Net Profit			10,500

(b)   Balance Sheet

Fixed Assets (FA : NCA = 3 : 1) (NCA = CL)		£52,500
Current Assets	£35,000	
Current Liabilities (CA : CL = 2 : 1)	17,500	17,500
		*70,000
Equity		35,000
Long-term Debt (Equity : Long-term Debt = 1 : 1)		35,000
		70,000

* Capital Employed
ROCE = Profit Before Interest/Closing Capital Employed
  = (£40,000 − £14,000 − £12,000)/Closing Capital Employed = 20%
£14,000 = 20% of Closing Capital Employed
Therefore, £70,000 = Closing Capital Employed

Suggested Solution to Question 15.10

Puzzles Ltd.
Trading and Profit and Loss Account for the Year Ended 31 March 1997

Sales		W1	£1,200,000
Cost of Sales			
Opening Stock		£300,000	
+ Purchases		900,000	
		1,200,000	
− Closing Stock		300,000	
	W2		900,000
Gross Profit	W2		300,000
Expenses			
Depreciation (£600,000 × 10%)		60,000	
Business Expenses		120,000	180,000
Net Profit (10% of sales)			120,000

Puzzles Ltd.
Balance Sheet as at 31 March 1997

		Cost	Depreciation	NBV
Fixed Assets (Provision for Depreciation = 40% of cost)		£600,000	£240,000	£360,000

Current Assets

Stock	W4	£300,000	
Debtors	W5	100,000	
Bank [£480,000 − (£300,000 + £100,000)]		80,000	
	W3	480,000	
Current Liabilities (CA : CL = 2 : 1)	W3	240,000	

Net Current Assets (Fixed Assets at NBV :
Net Current Assets = 1.5 : 1)   240,000

                                                          600,000

Financed By:	Authorised	Issued
Ordinary Share Capital	£400,000	£280,000
Retained Profit for the Year	120,000	
Profit and loss account at the start of the Year	200,000	320,000
		600,000

Workings

W1 *Sales*
Ratio of Sales for the year to year-end capital employed was 2 : 1
Capital Employed per Balance Sheet = £600,000
Therefore, Sales for the year = £600,000 × 2 = £1,200,000

W2 *Gross Profit and Cost of Sales*
Mark-Up on Cost = 33 1/3% or 1/3
Therefore, Margin = 1/4
Margin = Gross Profit/Sales
1/4 (Sales) = Gross Profit
1/4 (1,200,000) = Gross Profit = £300,000
Cost of Sales = Sales − Gross Profit = £1,200,000 − £300,000
    = £900,000

W3 *Current Assets*
Net Current Assets = £240,000
Current Ratio = 2 : 1
Therefore, Current Liabilities = £240,000 and Current Assets = £480,000

W4   *Opening Stock and Closing Stock*
Stock Turnover = Cost of Sales/Average Stock = 3
Cost of Sales = £900,000 = 3 × Average Stock
Therefore, Average Stock = [(Opening Stock + Closing Stock)/2] = £300,000
£600,000 = Opening Stock + Closing Stock
But Value of Stock at the Beginning and End of the Year was the same.
Therefore, both Closing Stock and Opening Stock = £300,000

W5   *Debtors*
Debtors Days Outstanding at 31 March 1997 = 30
Debtors × 360/Sales = 30
Debtors × 360/£1,200,000 = 30
360 × Debtors = 30 × £1,200,000 = £36,000,000
Debtors = £100,000

Suggested Solution to Question 15.11

To determine the Gross Profit Rate achieved in 1996 that is comparable with that for 1995 it is necessary to make adjustments for the various factors referred to in the question.

		Sales	Cost of Sales	Gross Profit
'Unadjusted' Figures		£960,000	£576,000	£384,000
'Adjustments'				
Note (1)	New Line	−100,000	−65,000	−35,000
Note (2)	Obsolete Stock	−5,000	−20,000	15,000
Note (3)	Half Price Purchases	−80,000	−20,000	−60,000
Note (4)	Seasonal Sales	−60,000	−40,000	−20,000
Note (5)	Damp Goods Destroyed	—	−30,000	30,000
Note (6)	Stock from New Supplier	−50,000	−30,000	−20,000
	'Adjusted' Figures	665,000	371,000	294,000

Gross Profit Rate = Gross Profit × 100/Sales
= £294,000 × 100/£665,000
= 44.2%

The 1995 Gross Profit Rate was £360,000 × 100/£720,000 = 50%

Conclusion
The factors outlined do not account for the fall in the Gross Profit Rate and further investigations are necessary.